CREATING SUCCESS

CREATING SUCCESS
The North Carolina Community College System

A Fiftieth-Anniversary History

Joseph W. Wescott II

CHAPEL HILL
PRESS, INC.

Copyright © 2014 Joseph W. Wescott II

All rights reserved. No part of this book may be used, reproduced
or transmitted in any form or by any means, electronic or mechanical,
including photograph, recording, or any information storage or
retrieval system, without the express written permission
of the author, except where permitted by law.

ISBN 978-1-59715-097-2
Library of Congress Catalog Number 2014940166

First Printing

Contents

Foreword ix
Acknowledgments xi

I. The Vision and the Visionaries 1
II. Laying the Foundation: The Industrial Education Centers 17
III. The Sanford Years: Opening the Door to a New Day 41
IV. The Early Years: Moore, Not Less 69
V. Expansion: Plateau and Progress 87
VI. Renaissance and Reformation 99
VII. Challenges and Changes 137

Epilogue 157
Afterword 161
Appendix A 167
Appendix B 173
Bibliography 181
Index 189

Foreword

This history of the North Carolina Community College System relates the coming of age and maturation of a public higher education program founded in 1963 by the North Carolina General Assembly. The system was launched fifty years ago by a handful of schools serving a few thousand students. The philosophical father of the system, Dr. Dallas Herring, predicted that within twenty years the system might have as many as fifty thousand students. Today fifty-eight colleges, some with multiple campuses, serve more than nine hundred thousand citizens annually. Programs range from literacy to technical education programs offering terminal degrees and professional and technical credentials to two-year college transfer degrees. From the beginning, the mission of the system was to provide job training, retraining, and general adult education for North Carolina citizens. The system has remained true to that founding plan. Contributing to that success was a local-state partnership designed to keep the colleges responsive to the adult education needs of citizens near their homes. Each college was locally initiated, has a board of trustees and is required to have financial support from a home county, especially for construction, operations, and maintenance of facilities. Students pay tuition and fees covering a portion of the cost. The state shoulders the majority of the operating cost, especially for salaries and programs. The programs of the several institutions are coordinated through the community college system and the State Board of Community Colleges. Clearly the North Carolina Community College System, founded in the latter part of the twentieth century and maturing in the early part of the twenty-first century, is a success story worth telling.

Joe Wescott's golden-anniversary history of the North Carolina Community System, *Creating Success*, will be useful to legislators, college trustees, state board members, college personnel, and students interested in learning about community colleges. His book tells the story of the founding and much of the first-half-century history of the North Carolina Community College System. We commend it to you.

    Ben E. Fountain Jr.   H. Martin Lancaster
    President Emeritus   President Emeritus
    NCCCS   NCCCS
    June 1, 2013   June 1, 2013

Acknowledgments

No one writes a book alone, and that is particularly true of this one. I want to express my sincere appreciation to the following individuals without whom this book would not have been written. First and foremost I want to thank Dr. Edgar J. Boone, without whose encouragement and support over the past several years, the book would never have existed, and indeed much of the historical scholarship surrounding community colleges in North Carolina would have been sorely lacking. I also wish to thank the members of the Fiftieth Anniversary Committee for trusting me with this important task. I am indebted to Mr. Clark Adams, Dr. Stuart Fountain, Mr. George Fouts, Dr. Herman Porter, and Dr. Raymond Stone for reading and commenting on the manuscript. Of those, I wish to particularly thank George Fouts, who guided this manuscript from its earliest days and provided encouragement and counsel at every critical juncture.

I am grateful to Dr. Scott Ralls, president of the North Carolina Community College System (NCCCS), and Dr. Martin Lancaster, Dr. Lloyd Hackley, and Dr. Ben Fountain, former presidents, for their insights and support. Governor Jim Holshouser and Governor Jim Hunt were generous with their time and perspectives.

I especially wish to acknowledge the assistance of the following individuals and institutions: Diana Zwilling and Melanie Clark, my research assistants, who were meticulous in method and without whose careful work this book would be less accurate and wanting in many ways; Bryan Jenkins of the NCCCS Foundation Office, who provided access to the community college system archives and assistance as needed; Dr. Carol Melton, who offered technical advice and encouragement throughout; Kennon Briggs, who shepherded this project through its early stages; and Edwina Woodbury, of Chapel Hill Press, who almost kept me on schedule and always provided excellent advice and counsel.

For their unwavering support and ready encouragement throughout, I wish to thank my parents, JW and Deloris Wescott, as well as Rob Worley, Mike Goodman, Tracy Clay, Nicole Schoenwetter, and Chad Nimz. And for refreshment of soul and body on many a late night of research and writing, I express my gratitude to Ashley Christensen, Matt Fern, and the genial staff of Poole's Diner in Raleigh.

Above all, I wish to thank my three children, Rachael, Joseph, and Rose, for enduring my absentmindedness and inattention over the past year as my mind was often away in the last century. Without your inspiration and understanding, this work would not have been possible, and you come of age in a North Carolina with a bright and unbridled future in large part due to the success of the North Carolina Community College System.

CREATING SUCCESS

I

The Vision and the Visionaries

Where there is no vision, the people perish.
PROVERBS 29:18 KJV

Dallas, his vision, came to see the public schools and then the community colleges as a way of reaching out to the non vocal people of North Carolina, the inarticulate people, the poor people of the state, the isolated people of the state, the women of the state, people who had in their chest the desire to improve, but didn't have a way. Dallas championed that cause.
RAYMOND STONE

Community colleges have forever changed the face of higher education in North Carolina. The community college system enrolls over eight hundred thousand students, many of them African Americans, single mothers, Hispanic Americans, first generation college students, and those who cannot afford more expensive educational options. Although the founders could not have foreseen the far-reaching changes that the system would help bring about, certainly they were not oblivious to the changes taking place in this turbulent period of the state's history following World War II and were motivated to prepare for what would come to pass. Foremost in the mind of some policymakers was the desire to create a system that would be accessible to all people.

William Dallas Herring, chairman of the North Carolina State Board of Education and a member of the Governor's Commission on Education beyond the High School, wrote to Chairman Irving Carlyle on July 11, 1962, "The people are hungry for education. How else can we explain that in the space of three years we are reaching 25,000 neglected young people in the Industrial Education Centers whom neither the church nor the State was reaching before? No one has compelled them to enroll. They have enrolled because they need education for economic survival in an economy that is changing more rapidly than our ideas about education are changing."

The industrial education centers (IECs) to which Herring referred were a fascinating attempt to respond to a radically changing economy of North Carolina and to meet for the first time the educational needs of a large portion of its population that had been previously neglected and forgotten. Thousands of citizens, young and old, were being displaced from the farms and agricultural jobs where they traditionally scratched out a living. The few jobs available to unskilled laborers, such as those offered in the textile industry, paid limited wages. In addition, rapid and extensive social change brought about new demands for education and training for women and minorities. By serving this student population—whether old or new—the IECs became the foundation and future financiers for the fast-moving expansion of higher education in the latter half of the twentieth century.

After World War II, North Carolina remained primarily a rural state with an economy in which agricultural enterprises played a major role. In 1940, as reported in the U.S. Census, 33.6 percent of North Carolina's workforce was in agriculture, and most resided in the eastern part of the state. Yet the rapid growth of industry stimulated nationally by World War II greatly affected North Carolinians. This industrialization, combined with technological advancement and societal disruption, brought about demands for change.

The war effort had required a tremendous amount of manpower. Approximately 258,000 men and women from North Carolina had served in the army during the war. Another 90,000 served in the navy and 13,000 in the Marine Corps. Some 4,088 of these men were killed in action and never returned home. Many of those who did, returned to North Carolina with war brides from other nations or parts of the United States, and these women contributed to a more urbane attitude throughout the state. Many thousands of these North Carolinians also came home determined to take advantage of the educational opportunities afforded to honorably discharged veterans in the new G.I. Bill of Rights. Many wanted to improve their home or adopted state. As William Friday, former president of the University of North Carolina, remembered in 1999,

> This generation had a sense of morality, commitment, and honor. You learn these things when you are deprived yourself. You learn them when you go through a war where there's death. Where everything you do is to kill and destroy and to tear down, for a good reason to be sure, but your whole orientation is that way. When you've got all that behind you and you're lucky enough to get home, you're different. Not from any ego sense or in any vain sense, but you just know if there's something to be done, you're going to have to do it.

To prepare themselves, veterans returned to North Carolina and turned to the state's public and private colleges for the training that the federal government would now fund. Unfortunately, institutions of higher learning throughout the state were unprepared to accommodate the resulting upsurge in college enrollment.

R. Gregg Cherry, North Carolina's governor, urged leading state educators in 1946 to study the enrollment crisis. He appointed a steering committee and charged it with the development and implementation of a plan to ensure opportunities for a college education for all qualified applicants. The committee recommended the development of off-campus university extension centers at the freshman level. The plan was approved, and in the fall of 1946, twelve centers administered by the Extension Division of the University of North Carolina opened. In November the North Carolina College Conference (NCCC) approved the centers and lent them its support and sponsorship. The following year, 1947, saw the addition of sophomore courses at those centers that needed them. Simultaneously, however, C. E. McIntosh, the assistant director in charge of the College Centers for the University Extension Division, assured the NCCC delegates that "when student applications become normal, college centers will have served their purpose and, of course, should cease to exist." McIntosh's statement proved less than prophetic. The centers' influence extended far beyond their closing in 1949. Three became public junior colleges—Wilmington in 1947, Greensboro in 1948, and Charlotte in 1949—and they all served to emphasize the need for higher education facilities in North Carolina.

This need sprang not only from soldiers and sailors returning from theaters of battle abroad but also from the widespread changes in the North Carolina economy alluded to above. These changes occurred in a state that was among the poorest in the nation. In 1949, according to a 20 percent sample reported in the 1950 census, 65.6 percent of white families made less than three thousand dollars annually. The numbers for nonwhite families were even more unsettling. Over 90 percent made less than three thousand dollars, and of those reporting, 27.1 percent made less than five hundred dollars a year. The percentage of persons employed in agriculture remained high (24.9 percent). Of those employed in manufacturing (27.9 percent), the greatest number remained in textile mills (14.7 percent) and furniture and lumber/wood production (5.7 percent).

To understand what these figures meant, especially for rural North Carolina, keep in mind that, in 1950, more than 30 percent of all farm families earned less than one thousand dollars annually. Among nonwhite farm families, which is to say black and (considerably fewer) Indian, 60 percent earned less than one thousand dollars annually. The course of economic events, combined with racial discrimination, would force an even greater percentage of North Carolina's minority population to consider either changing careers or moving away.

From 1930 to 1950, 220,000 African Americans left North Carolina and headed north. Indeed, from 1939 to 1954, more than a million left southern farms for greener pastures elsewhere. Thousands of whites also joined in this migration. In a speech to the North Carolina Vocational Agricultural Teachers Association in 1960, State Board of Education chairman Dallas Herring pointed out that during the 1950s, over 40 percent (323,822) of the natural increase in the state's population "left us for greener pastures. It is as though the whole population of Charlotte and Greensboro had pulled up stakes and moved away."

Many of those leaving came from the farms. The rising cost of farming combined with declining revenues forced farmers, whether tenants or owners, to look elsewhere for income. Cotton prices were so low compared to everything else that by the mid- to late 1950s all but the few farmers able to plant vast acreage had stopped growing it. Cotton sold for $200 a bale; it cost $150 to produce and stood a better than even chance of being lost in the field. Corn rarely brought more than $1.50 a bushel, either in the 1950s or early 1960s, but it cost less to grow and was less a burden than anything else, so farmers planted as much as they could. Finally, because tobacco allotments were fixed, it was difficult to increase the amount under cultivation without incurring the cost of renting or purchasing someone else's poundage, if it could be found. Higher labor costs and rising prices meant that what an acre of land could produce was worth comparatively less and less. More and more acreage was, therefore, necessary to make a living, even though the more land a farmer tended, the more hands he needed to tend the fields.

The advent of mechanization only worsened the plight of small farmers and farm laborers. The mechanical tobacco harvester single-handedly transformed the growing and production of tobacco in the late 1950s and early 1960s, just as the cotton gin had revolutionized the agriculture of an earlier century. The effect on tenant farmers, white and black, was profound. As late as 1959, close to one-third of all farms in the state were operated by tenants. By 1964, only one-fourth of these farms were operated by tenants. And from 1955 to 1969, the number of black tenant farms decreased from twenty-five thousand to thirty-five hundred. As Dallas Herring, who resided in the East in Duplin County, saw only too well, "The age of the mule is gone. It is the age of science. The people must be given the chance to learn what this new age means for them, and they must have the education they need to make the transition."

Others, not necessarily in agriculture, found themselves trapped in low-paying, dead-end occupations. Throughout the state, but especially in the Piedmont and West, the stunted futures of entire families were tied to the textile industry. Victoria Byerly remembered,

> I had been a happy child living in my grandmother's house in the Amazon Cotton Mill village, but when I was seven years old my family moved to another town. Though my mother continued to work in the textile industry, we moved to a neighborhood where I came in contact with people who were not mill workers. It was at

this point that I began to feel ashamed of my background because I realized how poorly mill workers lived. We used outhouses instead of indoor toilets; we lived on beans and potatoes; we wore different clothes; and when the heels came off our shoes we hammered the nails down and went on wearing the shoes. In the mill village, where everyone lived this way, I had never thought anything about it. I didn't even know we were poor. But when we moved, I felt surrounded by people who seemed incredibly wealthy and who made me feel terribly inferior because of the clothes I wore, the way I talked, and the food I ate.

Life was often hard for the children of textile workers, and their opportunities were limited both during and after school. Crystal Lee Sutton of Graham, North Carolina, recalled,

Daddy always talked about education. He got real upset because he said that it didn't look like none of his children were going to graduate. So I was the first to graduate in 1959. The only reason I finished school was because of Daddy. I hated every second I went. I even hated study hall and lunchtime. I hated it because of the way the teachers treated the working-class kids. I resented that, because I didn't feel like we could help what our parents did, and I wasn't ashamed of my parents.

Sutton went on to say that she had really wanted to be a beautician after graduation, but "the nearest school was in Raleigh, and I just knew Daddy couldn't afford to send me because I would have to have a place to stay, so I gave up the idea."

The development of local education centers and colleges easily accessible to North Carolina citizens would change that circumstance. North Carolina had a long history of meeting education needs at the local level. Historians such as William Link and James Leloudis would later document the important role that local support played in public education in North Carolina and throughout the South. Indeed, this idea of communities meeting their own need for higher education through their own resources, or with limited state involvement, was not new. Nationally, the concept of public junior colleges—the precursors to the industrial education centers, technical institutes, and community colleges—had a history dating back to the turn of the century. In 1900, the University of Chicago, under the able leadership of William Rainey Harper, began awarding the associate of arts degree to those students completing its two-year "junior college" program. The following year, 1901, saw the addition of this junior college program to the high school program in Joliet, Illinois. The result was Joliet Junior College.

In 1910 the second junior college was established in Fresno. In California the public junior college had Dean Alexis F. Lange of the University of California as one of its most eloquent spokesmen. He and others saw the need for broadening the curriculum to include vocational and technical training. He wrote, "The junior college cannot make preparation for the University its excuse for being.... The junior college will function adequately only if its first concern is with those who will go no further, if it meets local needs efficiently, if it trains an increasing number in vocations for which training has not hitherto been afforded by our school system." In the years that followed, occupational education rapidly expanded in many junior colleges. This was encouraged by several factors. Unemployment during the Depression necessitated training for new jobs as they became available. Increasing mechanization of production, especially during World War II, required workers with higher levels of technical skills. Finally, as early as 1917, Congress had passed legislation such as the Smith-Hughes Act stressing vocational education.

The Smith-Hughes Act grew out of the efforts of the Wilson administration on behalf of vocational education. In 1914 President Woodrow Wilson appointed a commission that discovered that too many youth left school to enter low-grade skilled and unskilled industries that provided little or no opportunity for better wages or for promotion to a more desirable job. Those few adolescents who rose to success did so in ways that were wasteful to them and to industry. After repeated prodding from President Wilson, and a final lobbying push from the U.S. Chamber of Commerce, Congress provided federal grants for vocational education through the Smith-Hughes Act of 1917. The act stipulated that participating states set up a state board to administer the programs provided. The act also made available federal monies, to be matched by the state or local communities, to pay "the salaries of teachers, supervisors, and directors of agricultural subjects, and teachers of trade, home economics, and industrial subjects, and in the preparation of teachers" of these subjects. Over the next three decades, the federal government nurtured vocational education programs through regular, albeit small, grants of aid. Not until 1946, with the passage of the George-Barden Act, did the next expansion of aid occur.

In the meantime and partly as a part of the expansion of higher education, the junior—or two-year—college movement continued to expand. By 1940 the number of junior colleges had risen to 610, and enrollment stood at 236,162 students. California had the most schools with 64, but North Carolina had 25, most of which were private, church-related institutions. The 1940s were a pivotal decade for the junior college. During this period, the transition to community college took place. As mentioned earlier, the G.I. Bill provided the financial means for enrollments to grow dramatically. In addition, a new initiative at the federal level, the Truman Commission, provided the conceptual foundation for the industrial education centers and the community colleges.

The Truman Commission arose out of private hopes and personal politics within the Truman White House. As the war ended, Donald Kingsley, an important advisor to the president, began discussing postwar educational needs with his staff. He suggested to John Steelman, a conservative assistant to the president, that President Truman appoint a commission to study higher education. Although the resulting council was evenly divided between public and private representatives, some National Education Association leaders thought that public education was not adequately represented. However, the charges have never been substantiated. The chairman, George F. Zook, was president of the American Council on Education (ACE) and a recognized friend of junior colleges, which were primarily private in that era. The report, published in 1947, made extensive use of the term "community college," thereby recognizing a change from the purely transfer function of the junior college. In order to accommodate students' needs, the report recommended establishing a large number of community colleges throughout the United States.

Early in the body of the report, the Zook Commission pointed to statistics from the U.S. Census Bureau showing that "the educational attainments of the American people are still substantially below what is necessary either for effective individual learning or for the welfare of our society." In 1940 less than 16 percent of eighteen- to twenty-one-year-olds were enrolled in college. And in 1947, almost 17 million men and women over nineteen years of age had stopped their schooling at the sixth grade or less. In that same year, over two-thirds of eighteen- and nineteen-year-olds were not in school. The commission concluded, "These are disturbing facts.... We cannot allow so many of our people to remain so ill equipped either as human beings or as citizens of a democracy." The commission went on to suggest in its report that

> the American people should set as their ultimate goal an educational system in which at no level—high school, college, graduate school, or professional school—will a qualified individual in any part of the country encounter an insuperable economic barrier to the attainment of the kind of education suited to his aptitudes and interests.... The time has come to make education through the fourteenth grade available in the same way that high school education is now available.... To achieve this, it will be necessary to develop much more extensively than at present such opportunities as are now provided in local communities by the two-year junior college, community institute, community college, or institute of arts and sciences. The name does not matter, though community college seems to describe these schools best.

The commission foresaw that these colleges "will have to carry a large part of the responsibility for expanding opportunities in higher education."

Community college proponents were quick to respond to the challenge. Massive expansion occurred in states such as California along with the implementation of entirely new systems in states such as New York. Moreover, the eastern and southern states began to catch up with the plains and western states. A spirit of optimism and increasing aspirations came with an expanding postwar economy; the spirit animated and guided a prominent educator in North Carolina, Clyde Erwin.

Clyde Atkinson Erwin had attended school as a boy in Charlotte and Waco, North Carolina, and had been a student at the University of North Carolina in Chapel Hill in 1915–16. He had served as a classroom teacher, principal, superintendent, and president of the North Carolina Education Association as well. In 1934 Governor J. C. B. Ehringhaus appointed Erwin to succeed the late Arch T. Allen as state superintendent. He would serve in that position for eighteen years, easily winning reelection each time he was a candidate. A gifted speaker, Erwin was tireless in attempting to expand educational opportunity for all of the state's citizens. In December 1946, prior to the publication of the Zook Commission report, Erwin asked the State Board of Education to "consider and ponder" the establishment of community junior colleges. Erwin argued that such institutions were needed to balance senior college enrollment and make it possible for parents to save tuition and residential expenses for their children. He also felt that while such institutions would allow more youth to gain a college education, these institutions would have to be more flexible, meeting educational needs as they developed.

In the Biennial Report of the State Superintendent of Public Instruction (1946–48), Erwin advocated the establishment of postsecondary institutions on the junior college level. He recommended that Governor Cherry appoint a study commission to make recommendations on education to the 1949 General Assembly. He wrote,

> In view of these facts, I believe the time has come when we should give consideration to the establishment of several State-supported institutions on the junior college level. California has had a system of junior colleges for several years, and a number of other states provide this type of institution. The development of such a program in North Carolina would contribute balance to our system of public education. It would make it possible for parents to save on college expenses, which are rising, since many students could remain at home and attend such an institution. The State would save in that fewer dormitories at State institutions would be needed. And many students not now receiving any college education would have the opportunity of obtaining the basic two

years college training ordinarily offered in all senior colleges. It is the business of public education to meet the needs for education whatever those needs may be. We have come to the time when we have got to consider the need for greater educational facilities. I recommend, therefore, that a commission be provided to study this whole field and report its findings to the next General Assembly for such action as may be necessary and desirable.

The State Education Commission was authorized by the 1947 General Assembly and Governor Cherry appointed its members early in 1948. Although its stated purpose was to study and make recommendations concerning the entire public school program of North Carolina, one of its sixteen committees, the Secondary Education Committee, stated in reference to community colleges in the final report,

> North Carolina now (1947–1948) has twenty-one junior college centers associated with the University. Only two of the junior colleges are public in the sense that they are partially but substantially supported out of public funds under school district management. In an increasingly technological age,... at least half of the youth who complete the high school could with profit to themselves and the community pursue advanced studies for another two.

In late 1948 the formal recommendation of the entire commission was published.

Even though it fell short of recommending a state system of community colleges, because it felt the schools should be locally supported, the commission did suggest that "provision should be made, therefore, to authorize the establishment of community colleges to be supported by local funds in communities where they can be established without handicapping the regular program, when enrollment (a minimum of three hundred students) is large enough to ensure that work can be offered at an economical cost, and at centers which are logically located to serve the particular area with a long term program.

The immediate result of the State Education Commission's recommendation was that two bills were introduced in the 1949 General Assembly to appoint legislative commissions to study the community college. Both failed to get out of committee. Erwin, however, did receive authorization to name a community college study commission. In 1950 the superintendent made his commission appointments. The members of the commission represented a broad spectrum of the business, legislative, and educational communities. Allan S. Hurlburt, head of the Department of Education at East Carolina Teachers' College, now East Carolina University, was chosen as director and thus gave his name to the commission and its report.

The Hurlburt Commission divided itself into several subcommittees to study specific areas such as philosophy and organization. These subcommittee reports, after modification and approval by the full committee, became a part of the final report. Over the next two years (1950–52), the commission centered its efforts on the region within a twenty-five-mile radius of Goldsboro to conduct a survey to determine the state's need for a community college system. State superintendents and instructional supervisors from other areas were asked for their opinions as well.

While the committee conducted the study, North Carolina's supporters of the community colleges and technical schools continued to voice their ideas about the need for these types of institutions. L. H. Jobe, an early supporter of Erwin's ideas for a state system of community colleges and editor of the *Public School Bulletin*, wrote in November 1951,

> North Carolina needs a number of two-year publicly supported community colleges. Such colleges could very well be supported jointly by state and local funds, with perhaps a minimum tuition charge.... Four-year colleges, in the main, train for the professions—engineers, lawyers, doctors, teachers, etc. There are many students who do not wish to enter a profession, but at the same time, feel the need of further preparation than the average four-year high school gives.... A community college would provide curricula of a terminal nature for [students] who desire training for vocations which require only two years for completion—business, trades, technical jobs, salesman, etc. Such a college would also provide courses for adults who would like to change their vocations, or to add to training received

on-the-job. The support of such an institution from the point of view of the student would be less in that he would commute to and from his home. Thus the plant would be less expensive than an institution where board and room are provided to a majority of students.

Likewise, J. Warren Smith, director of vocational education in North Carolina from 1946 to 1960, supported the establishment of community colleges for the purpose of vocational training. In May 1952 he urged,

> Publicly supported regional vocational-technical schools are needed in this state to provide effectively those types of training which are not feasible in our present organization. For the rural boys and girls... there is no provision for instruction leading to the development of technical skills except that taught in the farm shops, which is for those boys who plan to be farmers.... Because of the rapid changes toward mechanization in farming, it must be recognized that probably not more than half of the rural boys and girls now living in rural communities will be needed on the farm. For these rural and urban boys and girls who at present do not have available to them the specific vocational courses they should have, some suitable type of school should be provided.

In October 1952 the Hurlburt Commission published its report, *The Community College Study*. The first state publication to be concerned solely with community colleges, the report advocated a statewide system of tuition-free, comprehensive community colleges. The first seven chapters of the report defined the nature, purpose, organization, and plan of implementation for the system in North Carolina. The report stated,

> The purpose of the community college is to offer educational services to the entire community, and this requires of it a variety of functions and programs. It will provide education for youth of the community and it will serve as an active center for adult education.... [It] should provide curricula and services of the following types:

a. A two year academic program...
b. General education program...
c. Terminal courses for vocational, vocational-technical and semi-professional training...
d. In-service training to help people already employed...
e. Leisure-time education and services, especially for adults.
f. Educational opportunity for school "drop-outs" to help them overcome their educational deficiencies.

The report went on to state that this instruction should be accomplished through local initiative, responsibility, and control and with a very low cost to the student. (It was suggested that students should not be expected to pay more than fifty dollars per year, and the remaining cost would be split evenly between the state and the local district.) However, the study was careful to point out that no institution should be awarded to an area unless it had demonstrated its initiative and commitment to the community college concept by "donation of the initial plant site." The study then concluded by outlining a plan for the 1953 General Assembly to follow to "authorize the creation, establishment, and operation of [a state system of] community colleges."

The Community College Study was a reflection of the views of Clyde Erwin and his consultant, Allan Hurlburt. They both viewed the system as an upward extension of the public school system through the fourteenth grade. They saw the community college as a means of alleviating such statewide socially stigmatizing circumstances as a high illiteracy rate and a low percentage of college-age youth actually enrolled in college. Strongly influenced by the report of the Truman Commission, the Hurlburt report embraced the idea of almost tuition-free community colleges with comprehensive curriculums that would provide for a wide variety of student needs. A major reason for the low tuition recommendation was the economic barrier that both commissions saw as the greatest single deterrent to a college education for youth who might otherwise profit from it.

Representative Roy Taylor of Buncombe County, home to North Carolina's first public junior college, set out to remove that financial barrier. He was a graduate of Asheville-Biltmore College and on March 3, 1953, he introduced in the General Assembly a bill providing for the establishment and operation of community colleges under the supervision of the State Board of Education. The bill also permitted school administrative units or parts thereof to consolidate for the purpose of establishing and operating the colleges and allowed the voters of the district served to approve special taxes to support the school.

The Taylor Bill, or House Bill 579 as it was then designated, emerged from the Finance Committee with a favorable report on March 19 and was referred to the Education Committee, which also gave it a favorable report on April 10. All looked well, but the bill was not to survive. Opposition to the innovative measure was led by one of the members of the Education Committee and a prominent supporter of private higher education, Roger Kiser of Scotland County. He felt that this new system of community colleges would hurt enrollment at North Carolina's private junior colleges. In 1957 most of these schools were affiliated with various Christian denominations, which helped to rally further opposition. Kiser insisted that the bill would "kick out of existence the church-related colleges in North Carolina." Kiser and other opponents of the bill also questioned whether the state could afford such a system of colleges. Since public education was segregated, Kiser pointed out that whenever one college was established, "You'll have to set up two of them." Kiser and his supporters were persistent and vociferous in their opposition, and although it passed its second reading by a slim margin on April 13, one week later the vote against it in the House was 62-42. The bill was dead.

One of the major and amazing reasons for Kiser's success was his ability to enlist the support of representatives from the rural districts of North Carolina. According to the *Raleigh News and Observer* (1953, April 21),

> Led by Scotland's Roger Kiser, the House last night killed the "Community College Bill."... Kiser arrayed representatives from sparsely populated areas on his side by holding aloft the threat of future State contributions to support the community colleges. And on the acid test, the small towners snowed under the legislators from populous New Hanover, Mecklenburg, and Buncombe.... Then the chips went down in the third reading. Kiser won a thumping victory.

Various reasons have been advanced for the defeat of the Taylor Bill. Two of the most remarkable are the voiced concern over extravagance and the predicted harm to church-related colleges. Other reasons advanced by historians and contemporary participants in the battle have been the untimely death of Clyde Erwin in the summer of 1952 and the lack of—or lukewarm—support from the governor's mansion. This vacuum of strong state educational leadership at such a critical time hampered any progressive change. In addition, the issue of segregation hampered any new educational ventures. Regardless of the actual combination of reasons, the state of North Carolina would now wait a decade before a system of community colleges could be established. There were some, however—among them a classically trained coffin maker and an innovative unelected governor—who were unwilling to allow the status quo of unmet educational needs to continue in North Carolina.

William Dallas Herring, father of the North Carolina Community College System, Chairman, State Board of Education, 1957–1977

Isaac Epps Ready, first NCCCS State Director (now president), 1963–1970

II

Laying the Foundation

THE INDUSTRIAL EDUCATION CENTERS

He who hath a trade hath an estate.
BENJAMIN FRANKLIN, QUOTED ON A SIGN
IN FRONT OF THE BURLINGTON IEC

And the greatest achievement was when we opened the door to the people who worked with wrenches and trowels, hammers and saws, the tools of working-class people. Universal opportunity for education as far as they could go.
WILLIAM DALLAS HERRING

On the second day of August 1956, two men who envisioned radical change in North Carolina's economy and educational system met in the governor's mansion in Raleigh. One was Luther Hartwell Hodges—punctual, precise, the fifty-eight-year-old former lieutenant governor who became governor upon the death of William Umstead less than two years before. The other man, whom Hodges had appointed to the state school board in 1955, was William Dallas Herring, a slightly built forty-year-old classicist who was already beginning to make an impression in the field of education. As Ed Rankin, the governor's private secretary, would later recall, "Dallas Herring was always around [during the Hodges administration]. Very prominent and highly respected, he and Hodges hit it off immediately. They both were businessmen, and they could talk the same language."

By 1956 Herring had long been active in politics and advancing the cause of public education. Having graduated with honors from Davidson College in 1938 he returned to Rose Hill, where he quickly became president of the family business, Atlantic Coffin and Casket Company. Less than a year later, at age twenty-three he was elected mayor of Rose Hill, the youngest mayor in the United States that year. Appointed to the Duplin County Board of Education, a position he had not sought, he found that he immediately disliked the board's method of serving primarily as a rubber stamp for the superintendent's decisions. He stressed more involvement and creative leadership by laymen and was soon elected as chairman of the board.

Luther Hodges was a graduate of the University of North Carolina at Chapel Hill. He had risen rapidly through the ranks of Marshall Fields to become vice president of the textile company. Retiring after thirty-two years of service, in 1950 he took a position with the Economic Cooperation Administration as chief of the industry division in West Germany. After working there and in several consulting roles he decided to enter politics and ran for lieutenant governor. He handily defeated three other candidates in the primary and went on to win the general election by a margin of more than two to one. He was sworn into office in January 1953 along with William Umstead, the newly elected governor.

Unfortunately, Governor Umstead did not like Luther Hodges and seldom confided in him. As Ed Rankin, who served as private secretary to both, recalled,

> They were not close at all. They came from different parts of the party. You have to remember that William Umstead was deeply experienced in North Carolina politics.... Mr. Hodges had spent his life in textiles.... He didn't really have much background in the Democrat party, all the functions and things, and didn't have any interest in it. He just wanted to serve, and he sought votes wherever they were. And some of the votes he sought were people who were actively working against Umstead. And so as a result, when Mr. Umstead was elected, he was very friendly to and he had a great respect for Luther Hodges, but he was not close to him.... There was basically a politeness or basically coolness."

Another of Luther Hodges's early frustrations came in the area of education policy. As lieutenant governor he served as chairman of the State Board of Education. He took "his position very seriously and he was not impressed with the way things were operating. The state superintendent of public instruction... tended to use the State Board of Education as just a sounding board. 'Here's what we're going to do, and then you approve it.' Hodges didn't buy that at all." When Governor Umstead died unexpectedly in November 1954 Luther Hodges was in a position to "purchase" a very different future for the state.

A moderate compared to other southern governors, Luther Hodges oversaw the desegregation of the public schools and the expansion of higher education opportunities. The former business executive and Marshall Plan administrator surrounded himself with a capable staff and focused attention on industrial diversification. However, changes in the educational system were required if his plans for the state were to be successful.

Dallas Herring had asked for the appointment with the governor on this steamy summer afternoon in 1956 to tender his resignation from the State Board of Education. On the way to the meeting he stopped by the office of a friend, Assistant State Superintendent of Public Instruction Allan Hurlburt, formerly of East Carolina Teachers' College, to discuss his intentions. Herring explained that he felt that he could accomplish more in education by resigning his position in Raleigh and returning to Duplin County to work with the Citizens Committee for Better Schools on the local and, eventually, the state level. Hurlburt, aware of the reigning status quo, did not discourage him.

Governor Hodges did. At the meeting, which was scheduled after the Board of Education session, Hodges asked Herring to explain his reasons for wanting to resign. He gently explained that he had grown tired of such activities as road trips to determine if anyone was cutting timber on land belonging to the state. Indeed, on one such trip with State Superintendent Charles Carroll and board member John Pritchett, he spent the better part of a day in search of Hell and Purgatory Swamp. (He would later remark jokingly that he had been to purgatory and hell with Charlie Carroll.) He saw such trips as doing little to advance the cause of education in North Carolina. He went on to tell the governor about the vibrant biracial citizens' movement in Duplin that had resulted in increased county appropriations for school buildings and the successful consolidation of fifteen schools. Herring also described his continuing experience with the national Citizens Committee for the Public Schools and how he felt this organization, working through the people, would eventually effect positive change.

As the conversation continued, it turned, as it often did with Governor Hodges, to a discussion of the governor's efforts to bring new industry in to North Carolina, from overseas as well as from the northern United States. Herring commended Hodges for his leadership, but went on to say that "it seemed...he was asking the impossible to bring in all these new industries to the state and expect the people to walk off the tobacco farms and go to work in the electronics plant without any instruction in what it's all about." Hodges, in turn, expressed his exasperation over the fact that he had never been able to obtain the cooperation of school leaders in such a training effort. He recalled that when he was with Marshall Field he wrote a training manual for textile workers and tried without success to get the local schools to establish a vocational training program. The two men then discussed the need for improvement in the public school curriculum, which both agreed had been neglected during and after World War II. Hodges told Herring that if he would remain, "I'll get you some help on the board."

The August meeting proved to be only the beginning of a long and successful partnership that would bring about radical changes in vocational education and eventually higher education in the state. Herring recalled later, "Luther Hodges and I understood each other and we hit it off.... We could talk business to each other. We were tired of the political and educational language and the reluctance to do anything about anything. Study it and never do anything about it. Hodges found in me a man who was impatient to get something done. I found in him a man who wished he had someone to help him get something done. So we agreed. We moved."

Actually three new Hodges appointees who would come to share Herring and Hodges's vision were sworn in on the board that same month. They were Charles Rose, an attorney from Fayetteville; Charlie McCrary of McCrary Hosiery Mills from Asheboro; and Barton Hayes, a textile manufacturer from

Hudson. These men shared Herring's desire for a more progressive board; two of them, Hayes and Rose, shared his alma mater, Davidson College. They, like Hodges, were convinced that the recruitment of industry and the education of the labor force were directly related, and extremely important, practical methods of raising the state's per capita income. They would be joined in the years that followed by such men as Charles Jordan of Duke University and Guy Phillips of the University of North Carolina. All would support Herring in the new venture to train industrial workers in North Carolina.

Not everyone in the state's educational leadership looked with enthusiasm on the new educational effort. Early and unanticipated opposition came from the author of the 1953 report, Allan Hurlburt. He was opposed to Dallas Herring's enthusiastic support and encouragement of Governor Hodges's interest in the vocational training centers because he thought Herring was selling out the comprehensive community college idea. He felt that a system of community colleges was much more crucial to the state. He said later that "Dallas pointed out to me that for political reasons there was no hope of getting the community college system and there was hope of getting the industrial education system. I yielded to his political acumen." Others critical of the plan could be found among the membership of the newly formed State Board of Higher Education. Created by the 1955 General Assembly, acting on the recommendation of the 1953 Higher Education Commission, the board was charged with ending unnecessary duplication of curricula among North Carolina's colleges as well as formulating plans for the predicted explosion of enrollment in higher education. The legislature hoped it would coordinate the higher education interests of the state as a whole.

The Board of Higher Education held its first meeting in June 1955. Governor Hodges encouraged the board to "go reasonably slow in the beginning" and that the objective was "to obtain as good an educational system as possible and secondly, to do it as cheaply as we can." The agency was made up of nine members appointed by the governor with the consent of the General Assembly. No member was to act as the representative of any particular institution. At that first meeting, D. Hiden Ramsey was elected chairman. He proved to be an avid supporter of traditional college education and equally suspicious of post–high school vocational training.

Soon after his election to the chairmanship, Ramsey began advocating the development of tax-supported junior colleges, which he and others referred to as "community colleges." He stressed the monetary savings that would result from having these schools provide the first two years of college training. Speaking to the Charlotte Rotary Club in the spring of 1956 he stated, "The single advantage of such institutions is that they provide college training at the lowest possible cost to the state and to the student.... It is a demonstrable fact that students attend an institution in direct ratio to their proximity to it. Does the state have any responsibility to organize its system of higher education in such a way that colleges are brought within the geographic reach of its youth?"

Chairman Ramsey felt that it did. However, he was joined by the board's new director, Harris Purks, in his belief that such responsibility did not extend to vocational and technical training. In the August 1956 meeting of the Board of Higher Education, Purks suggested that the state should not support as higher education "any additional vocational or occupational training program which cannot be clearly defined as higher education." He said that there was already too much emphasis upon vocational education and that this type of training constitutes a "phase of education which is subject to overproduction."

As a result of such thinking, the board recommended to the 1957 General Assembly a measure providing for a statewide plan of organization for academically oriented public junior colleges that did not encompass vocational training. The legislature complied with the recommendation, and the erroneously named Community College Act was passed virtually without opposition. Although it provided for substantially more state aid for the existing public junior colleges—Asheville, Wilmington, and Charlotte—it required them to relinquish their administrative bonds to the local school boards and to be governed by a local board of twelve trustees under the supervision of the Board of Higher Education. Furthermore, the act provided no financial support for vocational and adult education programs. Finally, the support provided by the state was severely limited. Fees at the public junior colleges came to be greater than those charged at either the University of North Carolina or any of the other four-year state colleges. As a result of this flawed legislation, the growth of public community colleges was extremely slow; by 1962, only two colleges had been chartered under the 1957 law.

One member of the Board of Higher Education who was not pleased with the possibilities of the 1957 Community College Act was its most junior member, William Dallas Herring. Appointed to the board in June 1956 by Governor Hodges, he soon took issue with Ramsey and Purks over the place of vocational training in the state's educational system, especially in the community college curriculum. On April 16, 1957, he wrote to Gerald Cowan, an officer with Wachovia Bank and Trust Company and a member of the State Board of Education,

> Thank you for the clipping about the new metal-working plant interested in Black Mountain and the possibility of training the personnel needed. This was such a good case in point that I sent the clipping onto Governor Hodges with a letter about it. I feel we absolutely must do something about the need for training an adequate labor force as our industry grows—and I am not talking about the kind of piddling that goes on in our agriculture shops.... On the Board of Higher Education I have been plugging for this type of training in the community colleges, but I have gotten nowhere there either.

The young board member would have more success in his efforts with the State Board of Education, but not without having to overcome the initial disinterest and suspicion of some senior members. After returning from his meeting with Hodges, Herring began to focus much of his efforts on vocational training. Hence, it was the Community College Committee of the Board of Higher Education and the Committee on Professional Services of the State Board of Education that conducted a joint study of the technical training problem in North Carolina. They first accepted J. Warren Smith's recommendation to request $1 million for the program. After State Superintendent Carroll insisted that twice that amount was needed, they increased the request to $2 million. Early on, Herring feared the proposal would be derailed by opposition forces. On February 11, 1957, he wrote Guy Phillips and shared his fears that some were attempting to derail the proposal. He reported,

> Brower [chairman of the board] is sick again, so Pritchett and Carroll took the whole Vocational-Technical School matter away from the Committee on Professional Services, to whom Brower had assigned it, and appointed a committee consisting of Gill, Carroll, and Douglas to draw up the legislative proposals to govern the $2-million appropriation for this purpose which we have requested. I am sure this was planned. The whole proposal came from us, Governor Hodges and the Board of Higher Education. Dr. Carroll seemed to oppose it at first, but later insisted that Dr. Smith's recommendation of $1 million was only half enough. And now we have three men who were not really sold on the program to write the proposal for the legislature. Since I have said this much, I might also say that the Governor did not want the public schools to have anything to do with this program until I told him that we would personally follow up the matter and try to get the initiative in the department which is needed. Dr. Smith fully understands this, for I have talked to him and to Dr. Carroll with my customary frankness about it.

Two days later, February 13, Herring wrote to Edwin Gill, state treasurer and a member of the new committee handling the vocational centers, warning him,

> I personally discussed this matter with Governor Hodges and tried to incorporate his wishes on our proposal. Dr. Carroll's views, in my opinion, do not agree in certain substantial parts with the rest of us.... I do not favor an expenditure of this size if all we are going to get is simply more of what we already have. We need some realistic revisions that will result in an up-to-date program that will fit these students for gainful employment in industry.

Two months later, the vocational training proposal was still bogged down in committee. Herring complained to Gerald Cowan in April, "I have been trying my best to get some action on both boards about this, but Mr. Pritchett side-tracked me by giving the matter to Carroll (and we have heard nothing more from it since then).... I hope he [Governor Hodges] will help us out with this, because I know he wants the job done." That help would prove critical.

The proposal was sent to the General Assembly but immediately ran into trouble. Many state legislators shared Herring's concerns that they would get "simply more of what we already have [inadequate vocational training]," and the result would be a waste of the state's money. Therefore, on May 16, 1957, the Joint Appropriations Subcommittee voted to delete the vocational training center money from the budget. Two members of the committee—Representative Watts Hill Jr. of Durham and Richard Long of Person County—however, felt that the training centers might be needed. They alerted Governor Hodges, who in turn called Dallas Herring. Herring went to Raleigh to discuss the proposal with Hill and Long. As he recalled later, they went to the Sir Walter Hotel, and over dinner, Herring explained—at length—the need and plans for the training centers. By the time Herring left Raleigh at ten o'clock that evening, they had reached an agreement to attempt to get a conditional appropriation of five hundred thousand dollars to the Advisory Budget Commission. The commission would retain control of the appropriation until the state board presented an acceptable proposal, at which time the commission would turn the money over to them. The subcommittee liked this idea, and the appropriation was approved.

On May 23, 1957, Senator Long introduced a bill to provide for the allocation of funds for the area vocational schools. Strongly endorsed by the governor and supported by the Department of Conservation and Development, the bill (SB 468) passed its second and third readings easily and was ratified on June 12, 1957.

Events during the summer only served to strengthen Herring's concern for, and commitment to, industrial training. Also, changes in the state board's leadership served to strengthen his position. First, the requirements of the Community College Act of 1957, as previously mentioned, doomed occupational and vocational training in those institutions. On July 1, 1957, Herring wrote to L. H. Jobe, editor of the *Public School Bulletin*,

> I have felt that the ideal solution to the needs of these students (those with vocational aptitude) lay in a development of the community college program, which *can* have a good academic program as well as the occupational and avocational courses which most of these

students need. The Board of Higher Education has given grudging acknowledgment to this thought, but the control measures adopted by the General Assembly at the instance of Mr. Womble, in my considered judgment, will serve to discourage any enlargement of the non-academic program. I regret this exceedingly.

The loss of vocational training in the new community colleges only served to emphasize the importance of the plans for the new vocational training centers. In August 1957 Dallas Herring was elected chairman of the State Board of Education. In that position he could influence more substantially the board's direction and action. Under his leadership, events moved much more rapidly.

After the favorable action by the legislature and its departure from Raleigh, the State Board of Education spent the next nine months in intensive planning for the vocational training center proposal. On July 4, 1957, a special committee of the state board handpicked by Herring—the Committee on Terminal Education—met in Raleigh with Governor Hodges and interested legislators. The governor encouraged the committee to develop a sound, up-to-date proposal for the education of present and prospective trade and industrial employees, including mature high school youth. He also endorsed the board's request to establish a panel of leading state industrialists who would serve as an advisory committee to help fashion the proposal. Meanwhile the board moved forward in the establishment of uniform salary schedules and certification standards for teachers of industrial subjects.

Despite the fact that Carroll was asked to choose a professional panel to advise on the area technical schools, it was the Industrial Advisory Panel, meeting with McCrary's committee, that influenced the centers' development. On August 9 Herring wrote to the governor and explained his plans for the panel and the needs study:

> The meeting with our Industrial Advisory Panel was most interesting and helpful. I think it was significant that everyone felt we are not doing enough here and that our future industrial expansion depends in large measure on both the amount and quality of the instruction we do provide. Everyone felt we must expand

our program.... It is significant also that all of these gentlemen stressed the importance of a good, sound foundation in mathematics, English, and the sciences.

Events during that summer further ensured the presentation of a successful proposal. Herring began working closely with Wade Martin, the ambitious and energetic assistant to Murray Thornburg, state supervisor of trade and industrial education. Martin was convinced that the program would succeed only if "committeemen will take a selfish and specific view of their personal manpower needs" and suggested that the advisory panel include men who were mid-level managers (personnel director level) as well as plant owners and top executives. Two weeks after the July 5 board meeting, Charles McCrary and Wade Martin joined Herring on a tour of the trades and industries program in New Hanover County. Afterward Herring was even more convinced that Martin possessed the vision and vitality to head the new program. He wrote Hodges that the state board had decided that Martin should head the Trade and Industrial Education (T&I) section.

After the forced removal of the present director, Murray Thornburg, who was suspected of sabotaging the T&I program due to union sympathies, Wade Martin became state supervisor of trade and industrial education in late 1957. By then, the study the General Assembly had requested was winding down. It had involved a statewide survey conducted by industrialists and educators to ascertain the state's specific needs for vocational training schools. During that time, Herring drafted the proposal for the new institutions and suggested that they be called "industrial education centers" (IECs). The name, like the concept itself, quickly caught on. The state board was to vote on the completed study along with a corresponding proposal to be made to the Department of Administration at its next regular meeting.

Prior to the December meeting of the board, Herring mailed a confidential copy of the proposal to Governor Hodges. By way of explanation, he wrote,

> You are aware, of course, of the close study I have given to this matter myself for the past six months. I therefore want you to have an advance copy of the statement I have prepared for the

Committee to consider, although it may differ in some respects from the one to be presented to the staff.... For this reason I hope you will not mention that I have written such a statement and given you an advance copy when Charles and I confer with you Wednesday. Perhaps he has more confidence in what Dr. [J. Warren] Smith will be able to do than I have!

The proposal, along with the study, was approved by the State Board of Education on December 5, 1957. The proposal set forward the purpose of the program "to provide instruction in the subjects listed below at three or more locations in the state—under administrative supervision of the local boards of education and the State Board of Education in buildings provided by the local community which may or may not be separate from the high school building." The courses listed were basic machine shop training; maintenance, operation, and construction of electronic equipment; drafting and blueprint reading; sheet metal work; welding; and other programs such as instrumentation, quality control, and tool and die-making—the equipment for which may be moved as needed into any area of the state. The classes would be open to adults and advanced high school students.

The proposal recommended that all of the five-hundred-thousand-dollar appropriation be used for equipment, personnel, and instructional supplies. The appropriated money would be used as a "challenge fund" to encourage local school units to establish centers. Facilities were to be supplied by local school units or districts that succeeded in obtaining an IEC. The allotment of funds to the school districts would be based upon rate of industrial growth in the community, industrial employment, trainable labor supply, job opportunities, community and local industrial interest, type of courses needed in the area, interest of local school officials, and evidence of financial support.

With the board's approval and the governor's enthusiastic support, the IEC program moved forward. Soon after the meeting, Wade Martin wrote to Herring, "I think the tremendous possibilities of offering a realistic program [are] sinking in everywhere, and it is only 18 months until we can look for a supplementary appropriation, providing the present pattern follows a course of wisdom and careful planning."

Herring, Martin, and the state board closely followed such a course. By the spring, the locations of the centers had been determined, and the resulting proposal had been submitted to the governor and the Advisory Budget Commission. The IEC program was formally approved on April 11, 1958. The plan called for the establishment of seven industrial education centers during the 1958–59 school year, which would be provided with over $2.5 million in facilities by the local school boards in the areas. The seven sites chosen were Burlington, Durham, Goldsboro, Greensboro–High Point, Leaksville, Wilmington, and Wilson. Most of these early centers were located in the Piedmont because that was where the most urgent demand for training existed. Eleven other centers were granted approval by the board, pending appropriation of monies by a future General Assembly, for the biennium 1959–61. They were Asheboro, Asheville, Charlotte, Fayetteville, Gastonia, Kinston, Lexington-Thomasville, Newton-Hickory, Raleigh, Sanford, and Winston-Salem.

The centers were to be operated as part of the public school system and administered by the local superintendents and boards of education. According to regulations published by the state board, local boards could only gain approval and funding by giving "evidence of need of a program by certifying to the State Board of Education the needs as determined by an occupational survey." The proposal would include evidence of sufficient financial support, prospective industrial interest, and a projection of enrollment that met requirements. No district received a center unless it could demonstrate a need for at least 15 persons a year in each occupational field represented in the curriculum. To ensure job opportunities for graduates, the regulations recommended that there be approximately 150 local craftsmen or technicians in each occupational area related to the curriculum. Reflecting the influence of the Hurlburt report of 1952, no tuition was to be charged, and the centers were to operate with an open-door entrance policy.

Not everyone was pleased with the program or the location of the centers. Just days before the proposal to the Advisory Budget Commission, Hiden Ramsey sent a copy of a state map upon which he had marked the counties gaining the early centers. He dashed an angry note across the top, "Really is any comment appropriate and I refer, of course, to the map showing the locations of the vocational education centers approved by the 'State' Board of Education. The program, as implemented by these decisions is, of course, dead. It is so stupid, so unrealistic." Herring quickly replied, "Let me hasten to assure you, with regard to the Industrial Education Centers, that you have been very badly misinformed." He then outlined the careful and meticulous planning and program that led to the original centers being situated primarily in the Piedmont. He then concluded,

> Now I know that you and I are not in complete agreement, fundamentally, as to the importance of vocational education. Our disagreement is cordial and friendly and I trust that it will remain that way, unless we can resolve the difference. It would take too long, and would try your patience too much, for me to repeat the arguments in behalf of terminal education below college level. But I would like to make it clear once more that I personally advocate it for two reasons: the needs of "terminal" students are just as genuine and just as legitimate as those of academic students and, secondly, we cannot do a good academic job in the high schools in a one-track, artificial situation under which we pretend that terminal students should be reading *MacBeth*, taking more of the teacher's time and talent than the gifted, when, as a matter of fact, those students need instruction in the fields in which they *are* gifted, as a supplement (not a replacement of) to the academic courses they can get. If we differ on this, then we must, but we shall do so with the same spirit which prompted you to send me that wonderful prayer.

Dallas Herring knew that he and Ramsey would never agree, but Herring refused to be untrue to his vision. He felt that the industrial education centers would one day provide the medium for instructing both *MacBeth* and metalworking. As he had written to Sidney Chappell, superintendent of Wilson City Schools, earlier, "We can... turn our attention to building up the Industrial Education Centers so that after they are securely settled in good programs we may gradually introduce other vocational courses and then some basic academic courses of a terminal nature. Following this it will be only a step to introduce college-level academic programs of a junior college character and then we will have community colleges after the national level."

From April 1958 until September 1959 Wade Martin, Charlie McCrary, Dallas Herring, and others worked feverishly to ensure that the new industrial training program was successful in every way. Those involved with the program sought equipment and instructors, set up curricula and centers, and solicited support in political circles and private industry.

In addition to Burlington, the State Board of Education had given its final nod of approval on April 3, 1958, for the fall opening of five other industrial education centers in the state. The $500,000 provided by the 1957 legislature would be used to equip the centers. The local units had agreed to provide buildings valued at $2,268,000 and equipment valued at $150,000. The centers furnished an advanced curriculum in trade and industrial subjects supplementing regular high school instruction but still considered below college level. Money for teachers came from the state's regular vocational education appropriations.

Originally Wade Martin had announced that the Guilford County center would receive the largest single appropriation. He said that Guilford's rate of growth had impressed the state board when it was evaluating sites for the new program. Because of the wide variety of industries in the area, the initial planned curriculum included more courses (twelve) than any other center. These included quality control, industrial electronics, draftsman, knitter fixer, auto mechanics, instrumentation, and machinist with tool and die. However, the Guilford center was originally housed in the old county tuberculosis sanatorium building at Jamestown. As this was not a new structure, it would be displaced by Burlington as Martin's flagship institution.

The other centers originally approved to open in 1958–59 were located at Durham, New Hanover, Wayne, and Rockingham Counties. In fact, the very first center to open was located in Rockingham County. The Leaksville–Rockingham County Industrial Education Center opened in May 1958. The governor and budget officials, including prominent legislator J.C. Eagles, added a seventh IEC, Wilson, when it became known that sponsors in the county would provide $168,000 for a building to be ready for use in September.

The curriculum established for the first seven centers reflected the vision of the founders that the schools would meet local needs. Thus, the courses offered were based on the needs surveys that the districts submitted to support their request for an industrial education center. Even though the schools often taught the same courses, such as industrial electronics and instrumentation, they also offered courses unique to their area. For example, both the Guilford County IEC and the Alamance County IEC (Burlington) taught supervision and auto mechanics, but Guilford, which included High Point in its service area, offered courses in wood and metal furniture and upholstering. The New Hanover IEC, in a coastal county with little heavy industry, offered instruction in marine diesel engines and carpentry-millwork. Rockingham IEC offered training in construction trades and textiles, and Goldsboro IEC (Wayne County) proffered radio and television repair. The centers were established from the outset upon the principle of basing their course offerings on community needs.

In seeking to equip the new centers adequately, Martin and Herring once again demonstrated their mutual willingness to use innovative methods. They were alerted by Colonel Preston Melton of the U.S. Department of Commerce that more than fourteen thousand machine tools stockpiled during the war were to be released through the Department of Health, Education, and Welfare (HEW) on a loan basis to train young people. Realizing that quick action could result in the industrial education centers gaining up to $3 million worth of excellent equipment, including sorely needed expensive machine shop and electronic equipment, they sent a telegram to Governor Hodges asking him to contact Congressmen Carl T. Durham and Alvin P. Kitchin. These men were members of the House Armed Services Committee and thus in a position to help with the acquisition. Herring also contacted L. K. Alderman, a friend from Duplin County who was in Washington as administrative assistant to Congressman Graham Barden, to solicit Barden's assistance. State leaders soon realized that it would be best if representatives from North Carolina went to Washington to meet with federal officials. At the invitation of Chester B. Lund, director of field administration for HEW, Herring, Martin, and McCrary went to Washington in July. Seeking to accelerate the machine-tool surplus property program in North Carolina, and to explore the added possibility of borrowing equipment from the industrial reserve, they met with officials of HEW and the U.S. Department of Defense, as well as with members of the North Carolina delegation to the Senate and House of Representatives. The day after the trip, July 22, 1958, the *News and Observer* reported Chairman Herring as saying that Chester Lund had praised highly the state's proposal for industrial education centers, promising "machine tools and other equipment with which to start seven industrial training schools in the state this fall." As then aide to Congressman Barden, Congressman David Henderson, recalled, "Congressman Barden, working with Senator Dick Rutherford of Georgia over on the Senate side and his colleagues in the House, was able to get the military to begin to move some of it [to North Carolina]. Stored away in the mines of West Virginia, some of it [the surplus equipment] had never been used."

After returning to North Carolina, the men continued to work through state and federal officials to obtain the needed equipment. They even retained the services of an attorney, Vincent Tolino, to explore the legal angles of the transfer of the surplus property to the centers in Charlotte and Winston-Salem. By year's end, their request was approved, and North Carolina became the first state to receive equipment on loan from the Department of Defense. Governor Hodges announced the approval in December. The result was that over $1 million worth of machinery was now available to equip the new centers.

As the centers prepared to open in temporary buildings in the fall of 1958, plans continued apace to build new structures. In Durham, however, racial tension threatened to derail plans for a new center. On August 20, 1958, Watts Hill wrote to Dallas Herring,

> As you can see ... the *only* way that we can have a successful bond election in Durham is to continue to operate vocational centers for *students* on a segregated basis in our local high schools. On the other hand, the only way that we can get the $350,000 Industrial Education Center bond passed is with the support of the Negro community which means operating an integrated center for *adults* only.... If it is possible, or if there are not overriding reasons which would make it inadvisable, it would also be extremely helpful to receive a statement from whoever is appropriate to the effect that operation of the Center for adults alone on a basis which would admit Negroes is *not* in conflict with the Pearsall plan [The state plan

that provided a means for local school districts to choose to remain segregated in spite of the Supreme Court's ruling in *Brown*.].

Before concluding his letter, Representative Hill asked Chairman Herring for the names of those in charge of the other industrial education centers so that he could call them and determine what they were doing about the race issue. In response to this request, Herring called Wade Martin's office in Raleigh to discuss the matter and found L. E. Spikes, superintendent of Burlington City Schools, there. Spikes attempted to call Watts Hill and then wrote to Herring stating that the school people in Burlington discussed the new program with "the Negro leadership prior to obtaining the Industrial School Center." They agreed to use the facilities together, although due to the nature of the courses offered and job opportunities, the actual number of African American students enrolled turned out to be very small. In the end, the Durham center, along with the others, accepted the state board's policy decision that the program would be operated on an open-door basis. This was to some extent a product of limited funding as much as changing social policy. As L. E. Spikes wrote to Herring, "I do not believe that your board could take responsibility of financing the present school in the white school, and in the colored high school plus the Industrial Center."

When the industrial education centers opened on schedule in the summer and fall of 1958, most opened in temporary facilities, such as armories and other abandoned state buildings, while bids were being let on new buildings to be constructed. The Rockingham County center was typical of the new institutions. It began operation offering training in carpentry, technical drafting, electronics (radio and television servicing), and machine shop practice with an enrollment of 143 students in preemployed training. Eighty-two students were enrolled in continuing education for supervisors ("upgrading training of a supervisory nature"). The supervisory training classes in human relations, textile cost control, textile chemistry, and textile electricity were held in the conference room of Fieldcrest Mill General Office Building and sponsored jointly by the center and Fieldcrest.

Each program of instruction offered at the centers had clearly defined qualitative standards. After completing the prescribed course of study, each student was awarded a certificate indicating the specific kind and quality of his achievement. Since most students had purchased required hand tools by the time training was completed and were available for immediate employment, industry enjoyed the availability of a pool of skilled workers soon after a course of instruction was completed. In fact, after completing technical training, students were provided with a complete and accurate report of local job opportunities to assist in job placement.

Immediate response to the new program was ecstatic. In the first year of operation (1958–59), the industrial education centers enrolled six thousand students—almost one-half of the total enrollment in the various types of trade and industrial education programs in high school in North Carolina during the previous school year (1957–58). These students helped make 1958 a record year in industrial development in North Carolina. That year, 423 new or expanded facilities opened, representing a record investment for those facilities of $253,074,000. This expansion provided for 21,757 new jobs and an annual payroll of $72,633,000. This represented increases over 1957 of 32.48 percent in investments, 34.06 percent in jobs available, and 35.23 percent in payroll. These increases in turn fueled demand for trained personnel and increased support for financing and expanding the new system.

Wade Martin further encouraged this expansion by using the new Burlington IEC as a place for promoting the new program and demonstrating the possibilities of continued state and local financial support. By September 1959, almost one thousand students were already enrolled at the Burlington center, which boasted twelve full-time and nineteen part-time teachers. Classes ran from 7:00 a.m. to 10:30 p.m., with courses offered in machine shop, auto mechanics, sheet metal, welding, knitting, machine fixing, industrial chemistry, and other related subjects. The curriculum was arranged to meet current and anticipated industrial needs in the Burlington area. The school year itself consisted of four consecutive three-month quarters beginning in September.

Close cooperation between the centers and industry was evident as well. At Burlington, officials with both the Western Electric Company and Kaiser-Roth praised the new educational endeavor. An official with Kaiser-Roth was quoted as saying that his company expected "to derive far-reaching benefits from the industrial education center. Training in looping, seamless machine fixing, industrial maintenance, machine shop, and supervision will not only help develop skills for people going into hosiery for the first time, but will enable present hosiery employees to qualify for higher-paying jobs." In fact, throughout North Carolina, industries demonstrated their interest in the new program by donating $107,000 in new equipment and promising $53,000 in additional equipment. This included sizable donations from knitting machine manufacturers, auto and tractor builders, and other major equipment manufacturers.

Student response to the new program was enthusiastic as well. Even with basic eligibility requirements set to assure student success, student interest in the program continued to grow. At the Wilson center, some students commuted as far as one hundred miles to attend classes. Demand at Goldsboro exceeded all expectations, and Director Marshall said he had never "seen such a craving for knowledge." Statewide enrollment in the IEC program nearly doubled in the second year of operation (1959–60), increasing to eleven thousand. In early 1960 Director Wade Martin told the *News and Observer*, "It's hard to believe, but the State's industrial education program is already larger than the programs of both the University of North Carolina and State College. Everywhere a center has been constructed the demand for courses has been greater than the supply.... Already we've offered 105 trade, industrial and technical courses—ranging from auto mechanics to tool making. And the response has been good to all of them." This growth was accomplished prior to the additional centers opening.

As early as January 1959 Dallas Herring had suggested that adult literacy classes should be organized in connection with the new industrial education centers. Another example of attempts to expand the curriculum occurred in May 1959 when John Hough, superintendent of Leaksville City Schools, requested that their industrial education center be allowed to offer a course in commerce. He projected that immediately upon offering the course, they would have forty to seventy-five students enroll. Although Hodges and others were uncomfortable with it, the idea of expanding the instruction beyond straightforward vocational/technical training was already spreading.

The new Burlington Industrial Education Center was the site of a major celebration for the vocational educational establishment in North Carolina on September 30, 1959. On that day, two hundred state officials and other guests came to Burlington to tour the new center. Erected at a cost of $1 million, the Burlington IEC was the first of the seven new centers to open that fall. All of them were designed to train students in the technical and vocational skills needed to take advantage of the opportunities afforded by North Carolina's rapidly expanding industrial economy. However, when the Burlington IEC opened, it was obvious that a large portion of the initial appropriation had been spent there. Martin had gambled on spending so much at Burlington in the hopes of reaping a rich reward of support from state political and educational leaders and assuring a solid future for industrial education centers and vocational training in North Carolina.

Wade Martin helped to escort visitors through the local center, and Dallas Herring presided at the luncheon at the Alamance Country Club. Speakers included Charles F. Carroll, state superintendent of public instruction, and Charles W. McCrary, chairman of the Committee on Terminal Education of the State Board of Education, who introduced the governor. In his keynote address Governor Hodges praised the new program at length and outlined its development, organization, and operation. He then pointed out that for a long time the state had needed an improved program of industrial and technical education. Workers needed to be adequately trained if the state was to continue to expand industrially. Referring to the thousands of young people available to meet the need for this industrial expansion, he stated,

> These people are in effect being denied a place in the economic revolution that is taking place in North Carolina—simply because up to now no adequate facilities have been made available to help them through this transition. All our efforts to develop a balanced economy and bring greater prosperity to the citizens of this state will have gone for naught if we fail in our responsibility to supply the means by which our people can adjust to the changes. I think it has been dramatically illustrated in the early stages of our industrial education program that the people of North Carolina are eager to meet this challenge. Those of us here—as leaders in education, government, and industry—have a responsibility to see that the people are given this opportunity.

He concluded his remarks by questioning whether the state was ready to derive maximum benefit from the IECs and industrial development. He stated that the only means of doing so was to establish industrial education centers throughout the state of North Carolina. He pointed out that in addition to the seven centers already in operation, eleven others were planned. In order to activate and equip these additional centers and provide needed support for the existing seven, the State Board of Education had requested $1,491,000 for the current biennium. Although the Advisory Budget Commission had approved the amount in full, they had made it subject to a vote of the people in the bond election for capital improvements to be held in less than one month. Hodges encouraged those in the audience to work for approval of the bond issue on October 27.

Response to the meeting and the new program throughout the state was very positive. On October 10, 1959, Herring wrote to Hodges,

> The 1950s are rapidly drawing to a close. It has been a decade of tremendous progress... but the watchword in education for the new decade ahead will be *quality* in education.... Consider what we all witnessed at Burlington the other day at the opening of the new Industrial Education Center. Here is a new program of high qualitative value that came about, because a few people had the vision and were willing to accept your leadership. It is, without doubt, the most significant step forward in quality education that we have yet achieved and it is just beginning. It will grow. In fact, the problem here may well be to hold the growth down, so that quality will not be sacrificed, since it is becoming such a popular concept.

The future would prove Dallas Herring correct in prophesying that the program had only begun and that it would grow. On October 27, North Carolinians provided the capital for that growth through an affirmative vote on the bond issue. And earlier that year, their representatives in the General Assembly had officially authorized and designated the industrial education centers as a type of vocational school that would be administered by the State Board of Education and local boards of education. The law, as approved, stated that the IECs would have as "their primary objective the provision of that phase of education which deals with the skill and intellectual development of individuals for entrance into, or [to] make progress in, trade, industrial and technical jobs." Funded and with its purpose codified in state law, the future of the new program was secured. Events in the political arena, however, would assure not only the expansion of the new system but its final metamorphosis into the system envisioned by men such as Herring and Hurlburt.

The Democratic primary of 1960 consisted of four strong gubernatorial candidates. Malcolm E. Seawell was attorney general of North Carolina and was supported by Governor Hodges. John D. Larkins was a Democratic national committeeman and a former chairman of the state Democratic Executive Committee. I. Beverly Lake, former assistant attorney general and former professor of law at Wake Forest College, was a conservative and a segregationist. Terry Sanford was a state senator from Cumberland County and former state campaign manager for Kerr Scott's Senate campaign in 1954.

With the support of a broad-based coalition that included the Scott family and the "Branchhead" leadership—supporters of former governor Kerr Scott: Charles A. Cannon, W. Willard Barbee, and O. Max Gardner Jr. Sanford was generally acknowledged as the front runner. As such, during the first primary, attacks centered on him. Sanford built his campaign around the concept of quality education and frankly admitted that he would raise taxes if necessary to pay for the cost. Sanford's message appealed to state voters with the result that he led the field of candidates in the first primary with an eighty-eight-thousand-vote plurality; Seawell and Larkins were eliminated.

Race emerged as a key divisive issue in the second primary. Sanford's theme during the second primary was, "Let's not close our schools, let's improve them." As such, he appealed to many educators and educational leaders, not the least of whom was Dallas Herring. Herring actively supported Sanford during his campaign. In fact, early on he had told Governor Hodges that "he [Sanford] was for education, and so I will support him." With that support, combined with others, Terry Sanford won the second primary with a seventy-six-thousand-vote majority on June 25. He went on to win easily the general election in the fall.

Shortly after his election as governor, Terry Sanford appeared before a regional meeting of educational leaders hosted by the Southern Council for Better Schools, the North Carolina Citizens' Committee, and the School

Boards Association at Chapel Hill. There he was introduced by Chairman Herring, who referred to him as the "happy warrior of education in North Carolina." In turn, Sanford began his speech by reappointing Herring—the first announcement of an appointment in his administration—to the State Board of Education. Sanford stated, "Dallas Herring has brought imagination and vision to the needs of public education and leadership equal to the finest in the history of our State. As we go into this New Day of achieving quality education second to none, North Carolina cannot do without Dallas Herring."

Sanford went on to specify that Herring would continue to serve as chairman. As such, the World War II paratrooper and the scholarly businessman would work together to bring to fruition a new day in North Carolina education, which included a comprehensive community college system.

Agriculture class at Catawba Valley Community College in the 1960s

Science class at Lenoir Community College, 1960

III

The Sanford Years

OPENING THE DOOR TO A NEW DAY

My faith always has been that the people of North Carolina are ready to go—ready to make this New Day of opportunity a New Day of achievement.

TERRY SANFORD

Terry Sanford was an activist governor. Terry Sanford believed that government could and should be used to meet the needs of people. And he believed that all it took was leadership and telling the people what they already knew, since it would better their lives. So he took this beginning that occurred under Governor Hodges and ran with it, so to speak. And it was during his administration, there was considerable expansion of the system.

ROBERT SCOTT

Terry Sanford's election as governor meant that the private dreams and public ambitions of many educators in North Carolina moved one step closer to reality. Sanford refused to be bound by tradition. He insisted that it must become a stepping-stone to change instead of a stumbling block to innovation. In his first major speech after his election, in which he announced Dallas Herring's reappointment, he outlined his educational program for North Carolina. He told his enrapt audience at the University of North Carolina at Chapel Hill that he had chosen "quality education as the rock on which he would build the house of his administration." He went on to say, "If appropriate education is to be available to a degree that our full potential of human resource is developed, then we need to expand community colleges and industrial education centers."

In their third year of operation, the industrial education centers were continuing to expand. They enjoyed the support of most private, as well as public, organizations. By December 1960, private industries had donated $385,000 to the industrial education center program. In addition, a number of corporations had sent representatives into the schools to serve as teachers or in advisory capacities. Public support, especially among high school graduates and adults needing continuing education training, remained high. Enrollment in the 1960–61 school year reached eighteen thousand.

Rapid growth and enthusiastic support meant new challenges for those overseeing the new system. Chairman Dallas Herring wrote to Charles McCrary in 1960,

> There are several questions now coming to a head about the curriculum of the Centers.... I am of the opinion that we ought to call in our Industry Advisory Committee and insist on having some professional school people join them. We must know where to draw the line consistently in the interest of the whole program.... There is the danger that public enthusiasm will run away with this program. In a way, that is what happened to the public schools in general during the '30s and '40s. Physical education, handicraft "art," field trips, etc., etc., moved in on the basic subjects, so that there was little time to teach the things that mattered most. Perhaps all of this was good and such a thing has its place, but the system bogged down, because no one took care to establish some basic policies guaranteeing that there would be no infringement on the time of the core subjects of reading, mathematics, history, science, etc. Let's don't let that happen to the Centers. I think it would be well to let competent industry representatives say to us, "Here is what industry wants and needs most in the way of instruction of its employees." Representative school people could say, "Here is

what we believe to be the training needs of the *individuals* in light of these industry job opportunities." Your committee [Committee on Terminal Education] could then weigh these reports and eventually establish the priorities and, if after study it is thought best, the cut-off points (bottom and top) which ought to apply.

The dichotomy that existed between the needs of industry and the needs of the individual would continue to plague the system's development and growth. Herring and Martin would lead the struggle to ensure that the training offered remained technically advanced and relevant to the needs of the student, not just to the desires of industry. Martin wrote to Herring that same year complaining about a course in textiles being offered at Burlington. He said that they would offer it as a compromise with industrial needs, but it was not the type of course they would teach on a continuing basis.

The number of institutions within the IEC system likewise grew. Much of this growth in the rural areas of the state occurred as a result of the extension center program. On December 9, 1960, Dallas Herring wrote to Charlie McCrary about the new extension class in auto mechanics being taught in Rose Hill on a cooperative basis by the Duplin County Schools and the Goldsboro Industrial Education Center. Seeing firsthand the great interest in the class, Herring wrote to McCrary that he was in complete agreement with the idea of extension classes from the industrial education centers wherever there was a "proven need for instruction at points too distant for adequate transportation." He reported that he had already discussed the idea with Gerald James, and he thought the program was practical and should be put into effect. As for the reason for doing so, Herring stated in his letter,

> I have long been troubled about the problems of the "displaced persons" of rural North Carolina—the young men and women growing up on our farms, whom the farms can no longer support, but who have absolutely no technical training for employment elsewhere. In my county alone we have had a net out migration in excess of 2000 during the last ten years, in spite of the fact that we now lead the State in agricultural income. They have left us because

our economy would not support them.... Our obligation to these young men all over North Carolina must be met. The question is: how shall this be done? Most of the rural counties, which are too remote from our 18 Industrial Education Centers, cannot justify the establishment of full-scale Centers, at least at this stage of their development. Yet this instruction, or parts of it, will be needed. I hope the Goldsboro-Duplin County experiment will show us whether it is practical to manage an extension class on a cooperative basis such as this will be. I see no reason why it cannot be done.

Charles McCrary agreed that it could be done. At the January 4 meeting of the Vocational Committee, the first item of discussion on the agenda was the extension programs. It won strong support, and in February 1961 the State Board of Education voted to allow extension unit courses to be taught where an institution was needed but the area could not yet meet all of the qualifications for an IEC. The three general qualifications that the board required for the establishment of an extension unit were at least fifteen qualified students, a satisfactory local building, and the ability of a sponsoring IEC to provide the necessary instruction and equipment. Explaining the new program to the press, Chairman Herring stated, "Some people now live too far away from a center to drive there easily. Under this plan we can take the courses to them. Let's take Currituck County, for example. If the people there demonstrated the need for a course in, say, automobile mechanics, we could send an instructional unit to teach the course. The courses would be taught only until the needs of the community were met."

The extension plan of the industrial education center program primarily aided residents in far eastern and western counties. The plan became a means of helping citizens in the lightly populated rural areas of the state. Extension units were operated by an agreement between the board of trustees of the sponsoring IEC and the local board of education. The extension program spurred the growth of the system, as the units later became industrial education centers in their own right. Indeed, later Herring would state that he invented the term "extension unit" in order to "throw the bloodhounds off course. They [the units] were embryonic industrial education centers." From 1960 to 1962 the state board authorized four extension units and two new IECs. In the west they were Ansonville (Anson), a unit of Central Piedmont, and Isothermal (Rutherford), a unit of Gastonia. In the east, the Pamlico extension unit was sponsored by the Goldsboro IEC (Wayne County). In Duplin County, the James Sprunt extension unit began operating under the sponsorship of Goldsboro (Wayne County) IEC. Pitt and Rowan Counties were authorized to start new IECs as well.

As the system grew, it continued to rely on flexibility and innovation to expand in the face of limited appropriations. Dixon Hall, first president of James Sprunt Community College, recalled quite vividly that the "old days were different. For example, H. K. Collins, former president of Durham Tech, drew up the floor plan for his first building and supervised its construction. Department heads in those days were known to teach forty hours a week as well.... In my day I would go out to the tobacco field. When the cropper came to the end of the row, I'd ask him if he had thought about going to school next term." According to Hall, during that time, most boards of trustees were made up of "hard-core industrialists"—people from business and industry.

Anthony J. Bevaqua remembered how the extension unit in Duplin County began. He said that, like most units, it started very small. The new programs began "not in big buildings, but in churches and prisons...you name it, whatever." He recalled that the first occupational program they had, the welding program, they had in "some sort of small basement. If I had gone down to inspect it, I said that I would have immediately shut it down, because it was such a mess. They didn't have any ventilation system. But they had guys in there who were welding. They were getting jobs. They were going to Norfolk; they were going down to Wilmington. They were going everywhere getting jobs."

John Tart, the first president of Johnston Community College, remembered some of the problems, such as personnel and equipment shortages, that came with the expansion of the system. He stated,

> I had a secretary and a business manager; those were the only people I had. That was the college. And we certainly had not done any planning. We hadn't had the time to. We had 125 people wanting to take electric wiring. I had one teacher. And we went out and we found more teachers. And those students, well, it

> took probably two weeks to get the teacher, kept coming back. They were patient. I remember one night we had, I'm going to say, twenty typewriters and there were twenty students sitting in the chairs at the table with the typewriter, and there were twenty standing up beside the typewriter—each one of them saying, "That's my typewriter." I walked in there and they said, "We have a problem here. Everybody wants these typewriters."

Tart went on to explain that by scheduling additional classes, he was able to manage the students.

As the system expanded into new communities, the curriculum expanded to meet the new needs. In 1961 Durham added a program for training dental technicians, and Goldsboro added a three-phase program for poultry field men. The curriculum grew throughout the state to include six major types of programs: machine operators, craftsmen, technicians, supervisory training such as job relations and cost control, upgrading classes for employed adults including color television servicing, and trade preparatory classes such as carpentry and pipe fitting. Ned Delamar, a former army officer and a representative in the North Carolina General Assembly who would play a key role in the passage of the System Act in 1963, recalled what happened at the Pamlico extension unit and at other sites:

> They were training people to be welders and bricklayers. These were some of the first classes. Then we began to move along and we saw the need for fire service training. Other programs or classes included new industry training, supervisor development training, electric line safety training, and seafood occupation training. That was one of the big ones, learning to pick crabs and filet fish, net making and mending, and marine technology. It began to move. Governor Sanford saw how much it was needed when he came in.

And Sanford quickly became committed to the expansion of the system.

Terry Sanford had promised to make the advancement of quality educational opportunity the hallmark of his administration, and he kept his word. In his inaugural address he stated that North Carolinians must be willing to pay the cost of providing "the quality of education which they need to keep up in this rapidly advancing, scientific, complex world." Sanford went on to say, "Quality education was the foundation of economic development, of democracy, of the needs and hopes of the nation. This is no age for the faint of heart." Sanford came to believe that one of the best ways to bring this quality education about would be to emphasize and finance what he came to call "in-between education." In his first budget message to the General Assembly, Sanford referred to the "nineteen industrial education centers which are contributing so much to the industrial growth of our state." He went on to ask for $763,000 to pay for additional equipment for the IECs. The governor felt that the industrial education centers and the community colleges (more properly referred to in North Carolina as "public junior colleges" prior to 1963) could best meet this need for job training and education. Some were coming to believe that these programs could better meet the need if they were combined into one system.

At the meeting of the Vocational Committee of the State Board of Education on January 4, 1961, the fifth and final item was a report by Wade Martin and Dr. Gerald James on their observations on the California system of community colleges. This report grew out of James's trip to California during the week of December 5, 1960, to attend the American Vocational Association Convention in Los Angeles. At the invitation of the state director of vocational education in California, James went out a few days in advance of the meeting along with eight other state directors of vocational programs. During those eleven days, Dr. James studied the California junior college system. He determined that these colleges were analogous to the combined industrial education centers and community colleges in North Carolina—in other words, comprehensive community colleges. As such, he stated in his report that it was his "basic view that the combination of area vocational programs and community colleges in North Carolina could be accomplished with great ease at the present time while both are just beginning. We certainly see a need for both in North Carolina. Can North Carolina afford two additional systems of education—area vocational programs and community colleges?" He concluded that a time when both programs were in their infancy was the optimal point to examine their "basic philosophy, objectives, and projected ways and means" and to combine the two systems into one.

Dr. James's prescient question was more aptly phrased than even he realized at the time. Contemporary events at one small eastern North Carolina junior college, combined with the fainthearted and frustrated reaction of the chairman of the Board of Higher Education, were conspiring to overtake his report and force the examination of all of higher education in the state.

The February 1961 meeting of the North Carolina Board of Higher Education was in an uproar. Wilmington College (one of five public junior colleges in 1962) was petitioning to be granted senior college status. Wilmington had first requested such a change on November 21, 1960, when William M. Randall, its president, had written to Harris Purks, director of the Board of Higher Education, and asked the approval and support of the board in conferring the bachelor of medical technology (BMT), a four-year degree. This led the board of trustees of the college to expand their considerations and to seek senior college status.

At the February meeting, the Board of Higher Education found itself confronted with a request for the change in status, supported by a detailed and comprehensive thirteen-page report titled, "Blueprint for a College." It included plans to seek enabling legislation from the state legislature to amend the Community College Act to remove the two-year limitation in the definition of a community college (Section 2a[2]), and to extend the power of the legislature to appropriate operating funds for courses in the senior college (Section 7a). The report went on to suggest that at the next general election the additional tax of two cents per one hundred dollars should be sought from the voters of New Hanover County. It concluded that all that was required for the county to proceed was legislation at the state and county levels.

Major L. P. McLendon and many on the board were frustrated and fearful of where such action would lead in the future. Would other community colleges, such as Charlotte in the west, join in the rush to four-year status? The board remained in session until late afternoon without adjourning for lunch. Finally Dallas Herring suggested to Chairman McLendon that the idea had merit but was premature. Herring recommended that the board propose to Governor Sanford that he announce plans to appoint a formal study commission to take a look at education beyond high school—specifically at community colleges. The board could then ask for delay in any further decisions affecting the organization of higher education in the state. McLendon and others on the board liked the idea, as did Governor Sanford when McLendon and Herring went to see him. Sanford agreed to appoint the commission.

Chairman McLendon hoped to get the Board of Higher Education to appoint the commission and thus effectively control its outcome. When Dallas Herring learned of this, he hastened to pen a letter to Governor Sanford, which he sent to Raleigh by Robert Carr, a legislator, on Sunday, February 19. He urged Sanford to reserve the right either to make appointments to the study commission or to approve the appointments to be made by the Board of Higher Education. He confided to Sanford that Major McLendon had only reluctantly agreed to have representation from public school leaders, who had a vital interest in the community college program. He concluded, "If we had made the right decision with regard to policy in this field in 1957, some of the serious problems now coming up probably would never have arisen. I hope that you yourself will give the study committee a well-defined policy directive as a guide for the study. You have every right to exert leadership of this kind and I, for one, desire very much to follow you and to help you in any way I can."

With this letter, Herring decisively outflanked McLendon and his mentor, Hiden Ramsey, the former chairman of the Board of Higher Education. At his press conference the following day, Sanford announced that he had asked the State Board of Higher Education to suggest names of educators who should serve on a committee to work out a long-range state policy for extending the community college system. Questions that needed to be explored, according to the governor, included whether the present community college law is adequate as an "instrument of policy; what should be the relationship between two-year schools and the non-degree-granting units of the expanding Industrial Education Center program; what should be the standards in determining need for additional two-year institutions, and what should be the relationship between two-year institutions and four year institutions?"

Later that year Dallas Herring and William Friday, the president of the University of North Carolina, met with Governor Sanford and Raymond Stone, the governor's education assistant, to recommend commission members. With the exception of three members, Sanford followed their recommendations. In

September he announced the members of the commission. Formally named the Governor's Commission on Education Beyond the High School, it came to be referred to as the Carlyle Commission, after its chairman, Irving E. Carlyle, a powerful attorney from Winston-Salem. Dallas Herring, who was appointed, and others would work through the commission to fulfill their dream of a comprehensive community college system that was initially established around the system of industrial education centers.

Although they continued to grow rapidly, the centers experienced a pivotal year in 1961. Two major setbacks occurred in the areas of personnel and funding. First, the new state system lost its innovative and energetic director to its sister state, South Carolina. Wade Martin was courted by the South Carolina governor, Ernest F. Hollings, who wanted to establish a system of industrial education centers similar to the one in North Carolina. In fact, groups from South Carolina toured the Burlington Center. Martin was particularly vulnerable because of his low salary, a fact that had concerned Herring for some time. As late as December 1960 he was writing to McCrary that Martin's salary must be increased at least 5 percent to $10,105. It was too little and too late. In July, in the midst of tremendous expansion and continuing triumph, Martin submitted his resignation effective September 1 to become the director of South Carolina's new Advisory Committee on Technical Education. His new salary was $14,400, a huge increase over what he was making in North Carolina.

Upon receiving Martin's letter of resignation, Herring wrote that he deeply regretted Martin's decision to leave, especially at a time when their careful planning and work "revealed considerable opportunity for service of unusual importance." He continued,

> I think I regret more than anything else the fact that you will not be here to enjoy the full fruit of your labor when these institutions will be junior colleges and thus full participants in the wonderful system we have dreamed of.... We certainly have not rewarded you well, but you will come to know, if you do not already know it (and I suspect you do), that the best reward is the knowledge that you have rendered service of enduring value to thousands of people of whom perhaps a majority do not even know your name.

Herring stated to Martin that he felt as if there had been a "death in the family" (personal communication, July 18, 1961, Herring Papers). Later, however, Herring would confide to Gerald James that the loss of Martin to South Carolina was not totally bereft of future benefit. He wrote, "Whether he realized it or not, I do feel that Wade did not have his heart in this and he (perhaps subconsciously) actually considered this broadening of the curriculum a threat to the industrial courses or his leadership. I say this without meaning to be critical of him." Herring had sensed that Wade Martin was yet to fully embrace the idea of the comprehensive community college and was not in favor of expanding the curriculum at the IECs beyond vocational or technical training.

No successor to Martin had been picked, and Dr. Gerald James oversaw the IEC program until Ivan Valentine came from the Burlington center to take the post. However, neither James nor Valentine possessed Martin's unique blend of vision and vitality, nor did they ever quite enjoy the close working relationship with Chairman Herring that Martin had cultivated.

The second major setback occurred when the state's citizens soundly defeated a bond referendum for capital improvements for the community colleges. Unfortunately, legislators had attached amendments to the bill covering many miscellaneous expenditures, up to and including toilets for Mount Mitchell. Another reason for the rejection may have been the amount of money that taxpayers had already spent at the local level. For example, Pitt and Rowan Counties had authorized, by huge margins, bond issues to build their industrial education centers. Herring wrote to John Sanders, the secretary of the Carlyle Commission, "I feel so blue this morning after the defeat of the bond issue that I am not sure just what to say to you about our plans in higher education. I trust that we will get over this defeat and will be able to win a victory eventually." Herring saw in the new commission a chance to fight for greater educational opportunities for the young men and women of the state.

Herring was determined to influence the commission to establish a system of comprehensive community colleges built around the industrial education centers. At its first meeting on September 29, 1961, the commission divided itself into seven working committees and named a chairman for each. President

Leo Jenkins of East Carolina College chaired the Community College and New Colleges Committee, and Major McLendon chaired the Development of a System of Higher Education Committee. In March 1962 the commission established a special study group on community colleges comprising these two committees. These committees had reported on February 23 that a professional survey team should be appointed in order to make recommendations concerning community colleges. This ad hoc committee, dubbed the College Survey Committee, was composed of Dr. William Archie of the Board of Higher Education, Dr. William Friday of the University of North Carolina at Chapel Hill, Director Bonnie Cone of Charlotte College, President C. Robert Benson of the College of the Albemarle, President Glen Bushey of Asheville-Biltmore College, and President William Randall of Wilmington College.

The College Survey Committee met seven times between March 8 and June 6, 1962. During that time, several consultants advised it. These included Dr. Allan S. Hurlburt of Duke University, author of the *Community College Study* of 1963; Dr. James L. Wattenburger, director of community junior colleges for the state of Florida; and Dr. C. Horace Hamilton, professor of rural sociology at North Carolina State College.

Dr. Hamilton had conducted a large number of sociological studies, most of which dealt with aspects of rural life such as tenant farming and health. The author of fourteen books and monographs by 1960 Hamilton had once stated that he was mainly interested in "getting facts into the hands of people who can get things done." His work became critical to the later success of the commission.

In the fall of 1961 the Carlyle Commission and the Board of Higher Education requested that Hamilton make a new study of enrollment projections for North Carolina colleges and universities from 1962 to 1980. The study impressed both commission and board members, and in early 1962 they asked Hamilton for a "detailed study of the entire State, by counties and areas, to determine the possible need for additional tax-supported institutions." This study, titled *Community Colleges for North Carolina: A Study of Need, Location, and Service Areas*, was published in September 1962. It documented an enrollment crisis in higher education and pointed to the need for state and private institutions "to move rapidly toward an expansion of educational facilities, if the needs of the state for the next eight to ten years were to be met." In the face of a growing population of college-age youth and the growing industrial needs of the economy, the study pointed out that North Carolina's fifty-eight colleges and universities were not distributed economically or conveniently in terms of either geography or population. For example, six large metropolitan counties claimed twenty-six of the fifty-eight colleges, and four other counties had one college each. Sixty-six counties did not have any colleges at all.

Hamilton suggested in his study that the best and most economical way to meet this burgeoning need for additional college facilities would be through community colleges. He stated that the "establishment of community colleges is an effective means of increasing the percentage of high school graduates going to college and of lowering the cost of education for those who can commute to college." Hamilton's in-depth study identified twenty-six areas in the state as possible locations for community colleges with a four-hundred-plus enrollment potential. These twenty-six colleges would serve a total population of an estimated 1,981,000 people. Their outreach and influence would be even greater if community colleges were established in ten additional areas having three-hundred-plus enrollment. Thirty percent of these students would not otherwise have an opportunity to attend college.

Hamilton's study proved to be a major factor in shaping the community college suggestions of the College Survey Committee. Irving Carlyle, chairman of the Governor's Commission on Education Beyond the High School, later referred to it as a "monumental job," and it proved critical not only to the committee's final recommendation but to defending that recommendation long after the commission's work was completed. The study also served to spur further expansion. After the study was presented to the committee and became public, many communities named as potential college sites began lobbying for a school of their own. William Archie's office was besieged by requests and letters, which he duly forwarded to the State Board of Education. These communities included New Bern, Lumberton, and Southern Pines.

Dallas Herring was undeterred in his devotion to the cause of expanding the educational opportunities for high school graduates and adults. Throughout 1962 he labored to have a community college system established, and he came to enjoy the support of not only powerful political leaders but most of the media as well. On January 22, 1962, he pressed his position in a paper titled

"Are Technicians People?" which he circulated to members of the Carlyle Commission. In the paper he pointed out the fantastic growth of the industrial education centers. He stated that the schools were reaching over twenty-two thousand individuals. As of the date of the report, there were twenty industrial education centers in various stages of development.

Herring went on to suggest that the state had a duty to provide educational opportunities for these students, which would meet their "*total* needs" at a cost they could afford and at locations within their reach. To do this he recommended that changes in state policy be made to allow the state board to develop a post-high-school-level general education program to meet the needs of these students. He also felt that the board should be given full authority to develop a system of credits and degrees for graduates of two-year programs offered by the industrial education centers, and the authority to cooperate with existing state institutions of higher learning in making extension courses available in the industrial education centers. Other recommendations involving administration, tuition, and standards and curricula were made as well. Herring concluded,

> We do not need and we do not *want* a society of technicians who have no sense of values in the realm of the humanities. We do not want a society of specialists who are unaware in a meaningful way of their larger responsibility to humanity, the State and themselves. But we do need specialists at the technician level. The important point is that we must not make them automatons, for technicians are people. They are human beings with human needs and responsibilities. The fact that they wear blue collars and come from less privileged economic groups has nothing to do with these goals, except to underline and reinforce the need for an intelligent and humane policy with regard to them.

Many people, including several in the media, agreed with him.

The press agreed with Herring's views on the need for comprehensive community colleges that would meet the total needs of students. The *Raleigh Times,* the *Winston-Salem Journal,* the *News and Observer,* the *Greensboro Daily News*, and the *Charlotte News* all favored the community college proposal. The

Asheville Citizen was typical when it declared, "In addition to eliminating a lot of expensive dormitory costs, this is a basic reason [convenient location] why North Carolina needs a number of good community colleges strategically located. The small colleges reach the people."

Not everyone eagerly anticipated the development of a community college system created by the merger of the industrial education centers and existing community colleges. Chief among these opponents were private college educators who felt the community colleges would be a threat to their schools through unfair competition for prospective students. Horace Hamilton had foreseen this concern and devoted a portion of his study to allaying private college fears. He asserted that although the establishment of new community colleges would have some effect on the enrollment of existing colleges—public and private, junior and senior—the impact would be mitigated by the rapidly increasing enrollment in all types of colleges. The competition between public and private colleges would be primarily on a statewide basis, as it had always been. In important ways as well, they were different institutions serving, for the most part, different populations.

Educators such as Dr. Budd Smith, president of Wingate College (Baptist), and Dr. John B. Bennett, dean of Brevard College (Methodist), disagreed with the Hamilton report. Both thought that private colleges would be seriously hurt by community colleges. Harold Cole, executive secretary of the Baptist State Convention's Council on Christian Education, warned that a community college system would "greatly imperil the private and church related junior colleges. Many of these fine private colleges will be forced to close their doors in the face of insurmountable competition on the part of tax supported institutions." In referring to the Carlyle Commission's work Cole fumed that the state should "refrain from the imperialistic policies that will force them out of existence." His concerns and those of Dr. Smith's would be amplified by a young media executive in Raleigh. Jesse Helms, vice president of news, public affairs, and programming with WRAL-TV, warned in a *Viewpoint* broadcast that fall,

> Governor Sanford and his associates have not even begun to prove their case [for establishing a publicly supported community college system]. They have not really presented much of a persuasive

argument for it. They have advanced an idea, undoubtedly with the best of intentions, but one based on shaky premises at best. This is as good a time as any for our legislators to remember North Carolina's motto which urges us to be rather than to seem. It is not enough to "seem" interested in advancing higher education; it is imperative that we "be" sure of what we are doing. It is important that we know the difference between ballyhoo and benefit.

Helms sought to cast doubt on the benefit to be derived from the new system as opposed to the damage that might be done to existing church and private schools.

Dallas Herring was certain he knew the difference between benefit and ballyhoo. In a letter to Irving Carlyle and in an article published in *North Carolina Education*, he eloquently and passionately stated the case for the new system. He began by recognizing "considerable opposition" among some of the private junior college leaders to the system of comprehensive community colleges. This opposition did not surprise Herring—after all, it had been the death of the 1953 effort—and he did not take it lightly. He called it a "modern expression of a historic argument" reaching back to the beginning of the twentieth century.

After complimenting the church colleges on their wonderful efforts on behalf of education in North Carolina, and pointing out that he was a product of such a school (Davidson), Herring went on to argue that a system of community colleges would neither damage nor retard "any worthy educational effort." Instead, it would actually reinforce and encourage the growth of all existing institutions because it would bring thousands into higher education who would not otherwise go to college and send a substantial portion on to existing private and public senior institutions. Beyond this fact, Herring warned,

> The State must educate. The State must be educated. The alternative is slavery—economic, cultural, social, and political servitude. The choice is between ignorance and enlightenment on a vast scale. If we do not double our enrollments we will double our poverty. If we double our poverty, we will double our dependence upon others and when we do that we give up that much of our freedom. The churches have no right to ask that we place a straight jacket on

public higher education in order that we may preserve the status quo at so high a cost in human value.

He went on to say that the twenty-five thousand students being served in the industrial education centers had enrolled because they needed education for economic survival in an "economy that is changing more rapidly than our ideas about education are changing." He asked, "Is technical education alone adequate for them? Are they not also legatees of our nation's grand concept of freedom? Are they not also inheritors of all that is great and good in Western Civilization? Shall we not teach them some of the humanitarian values that have made our country great?" He and his supporters were confident both of their need and the opportunity for North Carolina to meet it through a system of comprehensive community colleges.

While Herring was certain they must meet that need, others—and not just churchmen and their educational leaders—were not so sure. They, including some faculty and administrators at the state's colleges and universities, were concerned with the quality of liberal arts instruction that these students would receive in the new community colleges. An editorial in the *News and Observer* cautioned that community colleges might compromise their academic standards. The editor warned that nothing could be more tragic than that

> slip-shod, second-class institutions be established with the support and approval of the State of North Carolina. Certainly a fraud would be perpetuated on the hopes of youth if the graduates of the two-year community colleges were not well qualified to enter the junior classes of established North Carolina colleges and universities. And all State-supported higher education in North Carolina would be degraded if the State four-year colleges were permitted to lower their standards to accept poorly prepared community college products.

Chairman Dallas Herring, President Bill Friday, and Governor Terry Sanford sought opportunities to speak to university faculty and trustees and to allay their fears. In their eyes, the system was necessary for those whom the university often turned away and essential for the state's economic health. As Terry Sanford later stated before the University of North Carolina Faculty Club in Chapel Hill, North Carolina needed a system of community colleges that "will provide adult education throughout the State, which will give opportunities to those who would otherwise not have them and will take some of the pressure of numbers off the Consolidated University."

At its meeting on June 22, 1962, the Carlyle Commission unanimously adopted the community college report of the College Survey Committee. This document, which became a part of the final report issued in October, advocated a system of low-tuition, comprehensive community colleges that would be administered by the State Board of Education. That system would be composed, initially, of the twenty industrial education centers and the five (so-called) community colleges.

In a speech in Fayetteville, on November 15, 1962, Terry Sanford explained his plans to emphasize high-quality education at the college level. He began by stating that North Carolina must say to its young people, "If you have the will and the skill, you can go to college." His North Carolina master plan for education beyond the high school was based upon the comprehensive report that the Carlyle Commission had turned in to him some weeks prior. In referring to the industrial education centers he said,

> We already have in our state the community college concept and we have the industrial education center concept, having tried the former on a limited basis and the latter on a rapidly expanding basis. We know how these work, what they can do, whom they will reach.... This then will be our plan. One system of public two-year post high school institutions offering college parallel studies, technical-vocational-terminal work, and adult education instruction tailored to area needs, subject to state-level supervision by the State Board of Education, and advised by a proposed State Community College Advisory Council.

Thus the marriage of the industrial education centers and the public junior colleges was announced with the requisite rejoicing and weeping by both sides.

Neither institution would remain the same, but in the eyes of Sanford, Herring, and others like them, such change was necessary "to provide enrichment for the lives of those who otherwise would be passed by."

After the Carlyle Commission study was completed in November and made its way to the governor, Sanford wanted legislative action upon it in the forthcoming session of the General Assembly. He directed Raymond Stone to invite Dr. I.E. Ready, Director of the Curriculum Study; Dallas Herring, Chairman of the State Board of Education; A.C. Davis, State Board Controller; and Gerald James, Vocational Education Director, to meet with him in the governor's office as soon as a meeting could be arranged. The governor charged the four of them to draft a bill for early introduction in the General Assembly to carry out the recommendations of the Commission that dealt with community colleges. They divided sections among them according to their educational roles. Ready, a former teacher of English edited the draft for grammar. Dallas Herring reviewed it for content. John Sanders, a professor with the Institute of Government, applied legal language. Sanford charged Stone, "Push it through the legislature. I want it passed." Herring had won Sanford's full support.

As the draft bill made its way to the floor of the General Assembly, the Industrial Education Centers continued their spectacular development and expansion, creating greater access to education for students in North Carolina. It was a role that they would continue to play even after becoming, first technical institutes and then, comprehensive community colleges in the new system.

By late 1962 the IEC system had grown to include twenty institutions, the original eighteen plus the new industrial education centers in Pitt and Rowan Counties. In addition, four IECs were operating units that soon became centers in their own right: Anson, Isothermal, James Sprunt, and Pamlico. Altogether, the industrial education centers enrolled 25,800 students in the 1961–62 school year and 35,000 in 1962–63. In the 1962–63 school year, 3,240 students completed two years' training and entered career fields such as air conditioning and refrigeration, electronics, and mechanical drafting and design (IEC—Educating for Industry 1962, 1–2). In most areas, industry was anxious to hire the new graduates, and jobs or promotions awaited them.

Although the Carlyle Commission recommendations would assure the continued operation and growth of the industrial education centers under a new name, there was no assurance at the time that the important new legislation would pass. Referred to as the Act to Promote and Encourage Education beyond the High School (the Omnibus Education Act of 1963), there were fears among commission members that government leaders would give in to mounting pressure to avoid changing the IEC system and thus restrict its growth. The commission had made sixty-one recommendations for improving higher education, the majority of which were contained in the section titled, "Comprehensive Community Colleges." These institutions would be governed by the State Board of Education and administered through a professional Department of Community Colleges. A seven-member nonprofessional Community College Advisory Council would advise the State Board of Education.

The Carlyle report, as opposed to the 1957 Community College Act, stipulated that a district could be composed of more than one county, thus opening the door in many areas that otherwise could not support a college. Land, buildings, and maintenance cost would be borne by the local government; equipment, furnishings, and libraries were to be funded by the state. Two areas proved to be sticking points with some after the report was made public: selected industrial education centers were to have college-parallel instruction added, but only with the approval of the State Board of Education, and only after local interest and need were demonstrated; and these institutions were to be administered by a local board of twelve trustees, subject to the rules and regulations of the State Board of Education.

Early on, some commission members were concerned that Governor Sanford was uncomfortable with the idea of combining the industrial education centers and community colleges. On September 24, 1962, Herring wrote to John Reynolds, a fellow state board member, that he was glad to have his support of the community college–IEC concept, especially since Epps Ready and others had confided in him that the governor was lukewarm about this provision of the Carlyle report. Herring complained that he had written several letters to Sanford urging him to support them, but Sanford had not replied to any. Herring stated,

> The Governor said frankly that Governor Hodges had been pressuring him to refuse to go along with us on the Community College–

> IEC idea. He of course takes credit for originating the IEC idea and he did support it, but the idea came from us. I told Governor Sanford that I was never able to get Governor Hodges to see that the IEC students were entitled to some general education. He replied that he was strongly in favor of giving them general education, but he felt that Hodges had a point when he said that the comprehensive institution might have the tendency to lower standards in the college parallel work and raise the IEC standards too high. I told him that I didn't feel that this was at all the case and that in my opinion some of our IEC courses were just as high as much of the college parallel work being done in the senior institutions.

Herring stated that Sanford gave him the impression that he had an open mind on it and would be willing to listen to reason on the matter.

Neither Hodges's nor Herring's fears would be realized. Students from the industrial education centers were already beginning to prove the worth of their education. Within days of his letter to Reynolds, Herring had received a letter from Salvatore DelMastro, director of the Wilson Industrial Education Center, enthusiastically recounting how one of its students, Robert Collins, had "knocked the lid off" the college entrance exam for freshman entering the School of Education at North Carolina State. Herring was delighted and immediately saw an opportunity to press his point with Governor Sanford about the quality of the IEC courses. He wrote to Dean Durwin Hanson of the School of Education at North Carolina State if he would forward him a copy of the documentation for, as he wrote, "I think it would help me to convince him that our recommendation is correct if I could point out to him that we have achieved this kind of excellence so early in the history of the IEC movement." Such efforts and evidence proved successful in the end and won Sanford, if not Hodges, unflagging support.

Sanford, at the prompting of Herring, Reynolds, Bonnie Cone of Charlotte College, and others, became a staunch advocate of the Industrial Education Center-community college merger. As Herring and others had foreseen, Cliff Blue, Speaker of the House; Robert Humber, a powerful state senator; and much of the political leadership of the General Assembly quickly saw the value—politically and otherwise—of the new education system. Indeed, in those communities, which Dr. Horace Hamilton had suggested as potential sites for new community colleges, enthusiastic support was a foregone conclusion. By November 20 Herring was able to write to Bonnie Cone thanking her for her support and telling her that the governor had endorsed the community college proposal completely and was firmly behind the Carlyle Commission recommendations.

On February 7, 1963, Governor Sanford gave his biennial message to the North Carolina General Assembly. In his speech he outlined four objectives in higher education, which summarized the Carlyle Commission recommendations. They were as follows:

- A better definition of the university
- Greater cooperation with the private colleges
- Enrichment of the program at all state colleges and expansion of the university to include campuses at Wilmington, Charlotte, and Asheville
- Establishing—under the Board of Education and in conjunction with the industrial education centers—a system of comprehensive community colleges

To support his request for the new system, Sanford's budget request contained $1 million to make a modest start on the new system in the next two years.

On February 20 the Joint Appropriations Committee began discussion of the proposed system of community colleges. Two Republican members of the committee suggested that private colleges should be invited to give their views of the changes. Dallas Herring, appearing before the committee, assured them there would be no competition with private or church-related colleges. Irving Carlyle of Winston-Salem, among others, was invited to appear before the committee to discuss the proposal.

At the end, it was not the private colleges or their supporters, however, that posed the greatest obstacle to the bill's passage, but a group of public school superintendents and their supporters on the State Board of Education. These men wanted to retain control of the industrial education centers in their districts and felt that if they did not, vocational education would be harmed in their schools and redundant programming would occur.

As the IECs had developed in certain districts, a disparate emphasis had been placed upon high school vocational training to the neglect of adults for whom the system was originally established. Reid Ross of Fayetteville, Herrick Roland (and later, William Waggoner) of Wilmington, John Hough of Reidsville, Woody Sugg of Gastonia, and Craig Phillips of Winston-Salem had emphasized this type of training in their IECs at the expense of the adult education component, and in total disregard of the terms of the contracts that the State Board of Education had with their administrative units, which clearly required that the IECs were for adults. These superintendents could not bear the thought of losing control of the schools. In addition, some members of the State Board of Education shared former governor Luther Hodges's concerns that the addition of general education courses to the industrial education centers would compromise instruction in the industrial arts and cause the schools to lose their focus on vocational training. These members included Charles McCrary, influential chairman of the Terminal Education Committee; Charles Rose of Fayetteville; and at one point, Guy Phillips of Chapel Hill. Dallas Herring forestalled a direct challenge at the board meeting by meeting privately with Phillips. He later recalled,

> McCrary and Rose went out to have lunch together after the morning session. Guy Phillips, who was crippled by arthritis, went down to the snack bar in the basement of the education building. Aware of the simmering rebellion afoot I sought out Guy. Finding him eating lunch I sat down at the table with him. I reminded him that the Governor was firmly behind the proposal to merge the two systems and public opposition by Board members at this stage would only serve to embarrass him. Besides, I had the necessary votes to counter the opposition.

Phillips agreed to support the measure at that point.

Nevertheless, the opposition among the superintendents grew and solidified. Herring, always one to keep the governor fully informed, wrote Sanford on March 22 that a "minority of superintendents, who had IECs in their units, were disturbed about the Community College Bill." Although I. E. Ready had talked with them, he was going to meet with them in Raleigh at Fred Smith's office, Superintendent of Wake County Schools, on March 25 in an attempt to explain the advantages of the proposed system. Herring confided, "I am confident we can hold them in line." And in Herring's eyes, the March 25 meeting was a success. He was able to persuade most of the superintendents of the value of the new system to their communities and the state at large. He wrote to Guy Phillips, giving him a complete report of the meeting. He stated, "I think that Reid Ross and one or two others are the only diehards in this whole matter and that with the reassurances that I gave them ... we may expect this matter to die out without too much trouble." He felt this final threat to the system was over.

Unfortunately, Herring had underestimated his opposition. Still unsatisfied with the bill and Herring's reassurances, Reid Ross, William Waggoner of New Hanover, Fred Smith of Wake, John Hough of Leaksville, and others requested a meeting with Governor Sanford to explain their opposition. At the meeting, they again pressed the case that the changes would be harmful to vocational education in their units. Unknown to them, Sanford had earlier contacted Dallas Herring, who sat in an adjoining room out of sight, and heard their complaints through the open door. At the conclusion of their presentation and discussion, the governor thanked them for sharing their concerns. However, he said that Herring was in the next room and he was going to defer to his judgment about the matter. The superintendents left the office surprised and somewhat chastened, resigned to the fact that the industrial education centers would now become a part of the new system of community colleges.

Gordon Greenwood, Ned Delamar, and twenty-three other representatives introduced the Omnibus Education Bill in the House as House Bill 140. It easily passed the House. Delamar would later recall,

> We all thought it was a great thing ... Gordon Greenwood, who had the bill, Hugh Johnson of Duplin and a cousin of Herring, and I, we sat close together. Gordon Greenwood was right across the aisle from me, Hugh Johnson sat right in front of me, and Ed Wilson was just over the way. We got together and we got a

bunch of signers and we sponsored the bill. Clifton Blue was the Speaker at that time and we had it all lined up with Dr. Robert Lee Humber over in the Senate [Humber was chairman of the Senate Committee on Higher Education].... So while they were arguing about the name change of State College, we got the bill passed.

The bill was subsequently ratified as Senate Bill 72 on May 17 and was scheduled to go into effect July 1, 1963. After it was passed by the House and its eventual implementation was assured, Herring wrote to Sanford and stated that the new legislation "marks without doubt one of the major turning points in our educational history, an event which historians in distant times will cite as the beginning of what at last we may hope to call a true system of education." He went on to commend Sanford and other political supporters of the bill as worthy of the gratitude of all those "who desire to see the State reach out in a meaningful way to all who have the ability to learn."

The State Board of Education expressed its great satisfaction with the new legislation in a formal proclamation, specifically singling out the section of the law dealing with community colleges by stating that "all parts of the new blueprint are important and significant, but the State Board of Education especially welcomes the opportunity afforded to develop a system of comprehensive community colleges, technical institutes and technical education centers; and it is convinced that this new system, adequately administered and supported, will enable the State to improve its economic, cultural and social life in a way not otherwise possible."

To ensure such administration for the system, the state board named Isaac Epps Ready as state director of the new system. Isaac Epps Ready had graduated with honors from the University of South Carolina and went on to secure a doctorate in education from New York University. Four years earlier he had been brought to Raleigh from Roanoke Rapids where he was superintendent of schools, to oversee the State Board's Curriculum Research Study. As Ben Fountain, former president of the system, later remembered him,

> He was a very scholarly kind of man. My mother taught school with him before she was married and before I was born, in Rocky

Mount. He was superintendent in Roanoke Rapids, and I went up to talk to him as a young man about getting a doctorate. He did not encourage me. He was one of the few men that had a doctorate.... Then he went on to Raleigh with his curriculum study commission and was active in the effort to draft the Community College Act. Became the first director of the system. Just a fine scholarly gentlemen.

Ready and Herring worked together to oversee the development and expansion of the new system of community colleges in the remaining years of the Sanford administration. In addition, in June 1963 the Community College Advisory Council was established to advise the state board. Herring appointed Allan Hurlburt of Duke University to chair the new council. Other members of the sixteen-person body included William Friday; Bonnie Cone of Charlotte College; Howard Boozer, assistant director of the State Board of Higher Education; and C. C. Scarborough of North Carolina State. The new council was responsible for recommending solutions to the state board for such questions as "How should an open-door admission policy be defined?" and "How can the board equitably recommend expenditure of the $2.5 million expected to be available as general fund surplus on July 1, 1964?"

As planned, the industrial education centers became a part of the new comprehensive community college system. In fact, they were the primary institutions around which the new system was built. Only two community colleges operating under the 1957 Community College Act, Mecklenburg College and the College of the Albemarle, came under the control of the State Board of Education. (The other three, Asheville, Charlotte, and Wilmington, became four-year institutions.) Altogether, the state board was responsible for twenty-nine institutions.

The state board, acting on the recommendation of the Community College Advisory Council, established a policy for the transition of IECs and technical institutes to community colleges. Now the industrial education centers could begin awarding two-year associate degrees and be designated by the state board as technical institutes. College-parallel instruction programs were authorized in the institutes, which led to their status as comprehensive community colleges.

The state board decided to allow each IEC to apply for approval as a technical institute and, consequently, a two-year curriculum; the IECs were restricted to a twelve-month curriculum. In at least one case, Wake County, approval was denied until a capable president was employed.

By the end of the Sanford administration, the community college system comprised eleven community colleges, twelve technical institutes, six industrial education centers, and five extension units. In other words, in just eighteen months, the total number of units in the system had increased from twenty-five to thirty-four, and the number of comprehensive community colleges had increased from two to eleven. Furthermore, during 1963–64, over seventy thousand individuals enrolled in the institutions for short- or full-time training. Moreover, plans were afoot to offer a two-year registered nursing program, if the necessary legislation could be secured from the General Assembly.

However, a gubernatorial election would once again intervene to change the political atmosphere and give pause to community college leaders and their supporters in the government. Though Terry Sanford's anointed successor, Richardson Preyer, was poised to pick up the Sanford mantle of quality education, a quiet, thoughtful, and conservative judge from Western North Carolina, Dan Moore, was preparing to stride onto the political stage. In so doing, he would reinvigorate the hopes of the private institutions and church-related schools while requiring that the community colleges closely reexamine their growth and their goals.

Welding students at Asheville-Buncombe Technical Community College, 1965

Students in the Division of Nursing at James Sprunt Institute

Business class at Carteret Community College, 1964

IV

The Early Years

MOORE, NOT LESS

The only valid philosophy for North Carolina is the philosophy of total education: a belief in the incomparable worth of all human beings, whose claims upon the State are equal before the law and equal before the bar of public opinion, whose talents (however great or however limited or however different from the traditional) the State needs and must develop to the fullest possible degree. That is why the doors to the institutions in North Carolina's System of Community Colleges must never be closed to anyone of suitable age who can learn what they teach. We must take the people where they are and carry them as far as they can go within the assigned function of the system.

WILLIAM DALLAS HERRING

Understanding the problem of poverty is not enough. The undereducated must be educated; the hungry must be fed; people who are full of despair must be given new hope; and a new road must be paved for the lost.

FRANK WEAVER

"Stated briefly, my administration will seek to give the people of North Carolina honest, efficient, and economical government." With that statement, spoken at his inauguration on January 8, 1965, newly elected governor Dan Moore simultaneously described himself and the government that he would seek to provide North Carolina during the next four years. He went on to state, "I do not contend that we are a high tax state, but I do contend that our taxes are high enough and should not be increased." The governor went on to use the term "total development" twice in his speech, thus intimating that he planned to place equal emphasis on all services and departments of state government; none would be favored over the other. To careful listeners among the state's educational policy leaders, especially those in the community college system, the largesse of the Sanford years was clearly over. As Ed Rankin, director of the Department of Administration under Moore, recalled, "One of the things that he was hell bent on, he said that 'I am going to look at all of it. I'm not going to be the education governor. I'm not going to be the roads governor.... I will look at the whole of North Carolina,' and he did." According to Rankin, educators and the community college people no longer had an "in with the king."

Terry Sanford had tried to crown his successor and ensure that his legacy would continue. Former governor Bob Scott recalled that Sanford supporters held a semisecret meeting at the old Holiday Inn next to Interstate 85 for the purpose of determining whom "they would get behind and support for the next governor of North Carolina." Terry Sanford attended, though he donned a hat, raincoat, and sunglasses to do so. The attendees were led to believe that they were being asked for advice, but actually the decision had already been made. As Scott recalled,

> Finally somebody said, "How about Judge Richardson Preyer?" Well, that, you know, sparked some supportive conversation from Bert Bennett and a few other key people. So they said, "Well, let's get him in here and talk with him. We're here in Greensboro, and he lives in Greensboro." Well, it wasn't five minutes before he got there, and I knew he lived across town. So he had to be in another room down there. And they brought him in and anointed him as the candidate. And I turned around and looked at Lauch Faircloth and I said, "What do you think, Lauch?" And Lauch says, "He'll never make it in eastern North Carolina." And he was right. He did not. He may have eaten as much barbecue as anyone else, but he didn't talk the talk and walk the walk.

Opposing Preyer was I. Beverly Lake, representing the right wing of the Democratic Party. But the moderates and many of the conservatives in the party wanted someone in the center, who was neither liberal nor reactionary—someone to slow the pace of change. In Dan Moore, most felt they had their man.

Born in Asheville and a graduate of the University at Chapel Hill, Moore had served as a superior court judge and was renowned in the western part of the state for his fairness, honesty, and deliberate pace. Philosophically aligned with the conservative, established wing of the Democratic Party, his name was mentioned early on by his friends in the mountains as a potential candidate. Moore finally and reluctantly entered the race. Most political observers and most of his opponents' supporters refused to take his candidacy seriously. He borrowed the money from the bank to start his campaign, and his family made up most of his key staff in the campaign's early days. In addition, Moore was not a polished public speaker. Ed Rankin remembered, "In the early days of his campaign, when we listened to some of his recordings, John [Hardin, fellow campaign worker] and I said, 'Oh God!'... I mean, he knew the language, but he could not speak well."

But to those who opposed Richardson Preyer yet could not support Lake, he was their only hope. Lewis "Snow" Holding, a politically active young Democrat and prominent banker with First Citizens gravitated toward Moore. To Holding, Lake was frightening and Preyer represented more Sanford-style innovation paid for with taxpayer dollars. Rankin remembered,

> He got his crowd together and said, we are going to help this man. And one of the things they did was to call a rally of Moore supporters from around the state and have them come to Raleigh. They rented a bunch of buses and brought in busloads. Well, no one knew how it was going to turn out.... Snow and his boys went to work and on that night they had busloads rolling in from all over North Carolina to support Dan Moore at the big event at the hotel, and it was highly successful.

The result was new life for the Moore candidacy.

Moore went on to place second in the first primary on May 30, 1964, with 257,872 votes to Preyer's 281,430. With Lake eliminated, Moore could count on many of Lake's supporters to vote for him in the runoff. To the chagrin of Sanford and his supporters, some of whom tried to play the race card by suggesting Moore sought the black vote, Lake supporters voted for Moore in record numbers. Moore defeated Preyer in June by over 180,000 votes. He went on to defeat Robert Gavin in the fall by a similar margin, thus securing the governor's mansion for the conservative wing of the Democratic Party.

State Board of Education chairman Dallas Herring, like many Sanford supporters, had strongly and openly backed Richardson Preyer for governor. After it became obvious that Moore would be elected, he sent a letter to Epps Ready on June 16, bemoaning Moore's conservatism and expressing fear that progress in education could be endangered. He warned that his support of Preyer might result in his loss of the chairmanship and concluded, "I certainly intend to take a strong stand for continuing our present course [of expansion] even if I do not remain throughout the term as chairman. We could become the focus of liberal sentiment in a hold-the-line administration. If we do, we certainly must keep the issues, rather than the personalities, before the people. In either event, this job will require the utmost of us." As an example of the type of cost-conscious activities in which they might engage, Herring suggested to Ready that the department begin work on an in-house publication, *The Open Door*, which might serve to make the public more aware of the value of this new system of education.

As mentioned earlier, the governor's inaugural gave Herring no cause for comfort. But most startling to him and other community college supporters were the comments that the governor made in his first budget address to the General Assembly in March 1965. During that address, Moore stated that, in view of limited tax resources available to the state, the General Assembly should objectively appraise all budget requests and prioritize those that could be funded at the present time. He went on to say,

> As only one example, I would cite the community college program as a major area of activity which deserves your careful appraisal. Satisfactory progress appears to have been made in the new Department of Community Colleges. The General Assembly, however, must determine the rate of acceleration and development in this new field of state-financed education beyond the high

school. It would be well to reexamine the original concept of the community college program with reference to geographical locations, needs to be met, and the arrangements for state support. We must not overlook that North Carolina has forty-four private and church-related colleges which offer many educational resources that should not be duplicated by state-financed community colleges.... I should like to emphasize that I believe in the value of a sound, carefully planned, well-financed community college program. These institutions, along with existing private and church-related schools, can expand the reach of our educational system to many additional students and help take the pressure off our state-financed, four-year colleges and the university.

Obviously the fiscally conservative governor meant to look closely at the system's expansion, and private colleges and universities had a friend in the governor's mansion.

Dallas Herring was alarmed by what he read in the *News and Observer* the next day. He was even more certain that tight days lay ahead for the fast-growing community college system. He recalled that, during that same week, he drove to Raleigh to see state treasurer Edwin Gill. Herring considered Gill, also on the State Board of Education, to be an ally, and he was known to have the governor's ear. He was surprised to learn that Gill had actually written that part of the speech for the governor. Concerned that the system was growing too fast, resulting in needless duplication of programs and the waste of precious state revenue, Gill suggested the community colleges as one place where better efficiency could be realized in the future. Herring recalled, "Gill and I didn't fall out about it. He understood and respected my concerns that this was my baby and I was taking care of it.... I told him, 'You watch me and I'll take care of it. And Governor Moore won't have anything else to worry about.'"

Edwin Gill became one of the staunchest supporters the community colleges had in the new administration. Herring carefully courted his favor. He had his two field men, Ned Delemar and Ed Wilson, arrange for Gill and Herring to visit Wayne Tech. The state treasurer could thus see firsthand the work that the technical institute was doing. On the trip, Herring pointed out that the schools were teaching more contact hours in vocational technical training for industry than they ever had before. Furthermore, he pointed out to Gill, "You know as a scholar yourself that if these people can't read and write, they can't progress. So we've got to teach them." The state treasurer returned to Wayne Technical Institute in May 1966 to give the graduation address and to remind its students that "we must not forget that you cannot educate only a part of a man or a woman. What is done here affects the entire person and has its influence upon your total hopes and dreams." Gill was thus became an early convert to the idea of the comprehensive community college.

Even as he won new friends for the system, Herring was intent on gaining a measure of control over the system that would safeguard it in the future from such concerns as those voiced by the governor and his state treasurer. He had already grown concerned about the inequitable distribution of community colleges in the state. Also, there was no sense in the way that salaries were set. Some directors of extension units made two to three thousand dollars less than other later-arriving leaders. The business manager of Sandhills Community College was making more than the state controller, A. C. Davis. In some cases, the growth of extension units or new colleges was uncontrolled. As Herring remembered,

> They were growing like weeds in a barnyard hit by a little fertilizer. It needed to be, not muzzled, but put a harness on.... Russell Swindell created the one [extension unit] in Pamlico. I didn't even know it was down there 'til I went down to address the graduating class. I went down and they were all in the schoolhouse waiting for me to give out the diplomas. That's the God's honest truth. That's how informal it [the growth of the system was] was.

Herring and the Board of Education demanded that the department look closely at the growth and distribution of colleges and funds across the state. In October, the department shared its findings with the board. The results indicated that there were indeed some inequities.

The staff of the department had divided the state into three regions—east, central, and west. They found that roughly 34 percent of the total population resided in Eastern North Carolina, 51 percent in Central North Carolina, and 15 percent in the west. Yet, not counting extension units, the east claimed only eight institutions (technical institutes and community colleges), whereas Central North Carolina had fifteen and the west had six. The distribution of funds was even more disconcerting to Herring and others like him from the east. By 1965 the full-time-equivalent enrollment (FTE) of the system was 13,268. Of that enrollment, 42 percent were enrolled in the east, 50 percent in the Piedmont (central), and only 8 percent in the west—yet the Piedmont enjoyed over 66 percent of the equipment purchased since 1958. Most telling of all, the amount of money spent per FTE was much higher in both the mountains and the piedmont. It was apparent to Herring and others on the board that the east was not getting its fair share.

With the facts now out in the open, Herring directed the department staff to come up with a formula to determine how appropriations would be shared among the schools. He suggested that they take the line-item budgets and add up all the sheets for the whole system. Then by taking the FTE for each institution, they could come up with a formula. He told them, "We are going to have an equitable distribution of funds whether you like that region of the state or not. We're not going to pay more in Pamlico than we are in the Triangle. We might pay a little more in a metropolitan region."

Initially, there was resistance to the change. Herman Porter, assistant director, remembered that an institution's budget had previously been determined by a process of negotiation between the college president, his business manager, and the department, with Dr. Ready having more or less the final say.

During the rest of the winter and spring of 1965, the department worked on the formula. Herman Porter stated, "That was night and day. We would work on the formula, working on the paperwork. At night we would meet with people. A.C. Davis worked on the formula. I even remember in the midst of the formula development Dallas came to Lane Street one Saturday morning.... We sat down there in the library, Dr. Ready, myself.... We decided how much the supplies would be, how much travel allocation, details, details, details.... That was awesome."

Herring had stayed in touch with state treasurer Gill, assuring him that they were preparing rules for a fair and equitable formula budget plan whereby growth could be controlled and directed toward legitimate goals. Partially based on this, and on Gill and the governor's support, the legislature made the appropriation for the system.

Herring and the staff worked at a feverish pace on the formula for the next few weeks, and at the next regular meeting of the board in August, the formula was adopted. The money was released. Now funds were allocated to each institution based on an equitable and adequate amount in each line item of the appropriation, which was determined by the institution's full-time-equivalent enrollment of the previous year. The board invited personnel, institution, and staff to keep them informed of any hardships that might occur with the new system. They also created a standing Formula Committee to review the formula and make suggestions for its improvement. Its members represented large and small institutions from all regions, including Dixon Hall of James Sprunt Technical Institute, Salvatore DelMastro of Wilson County Technical Institute, and Richard Hagemeyer of Central Piedmont Community College.

With a new system in place to assure more equitable funding, the support of both Edwin Gill and Governor Moore was virtually assured. Also the department set about telling its story to leaders and citizens alike. The first issue of *The Open Door* was issued in 1965. It, along with future issues, attempted to illustrate and explain the great need for the new system of community colleges and technical institutes. The first issue included an article on the various academic programs, one reviewing how Central Piedmont had become a supplier of workers for the Charlotte labor market, and another on the use of learning laboratories in the new institutions. The issue also included a human-interest story, the first of many to be shared in the publication, about a mother from Fayetteville who had returned to school to better her life and that of her family. In that issue, Epps Ready stated the goal of the new system: "Any person who is eighteen years old or older, whether he is a high school graduate or not, can find in one of these institutions an educational opportunity fitted to his ability and his needs." Herring, in his inimitable style, challenged readers,

> During this century, North Carolina has consistently accepted the ideal of universal education, but it has not always supported the ideals which would make an education available on equal terms to all of its people. Possibly the cost of such an ideal is prohibitive.

> But the cost of our failure to provide, and the failure of individuals to achieve total education far exceeds the cost of the ideal.... So let us tear down the fences and open the golden door—not with vengeance or with malice, but with determination to achieve the goal of total education.

With the support of the new administration and the General Assembly, the growth of the community college system continued. In 1965, new technical institutes had been approved for Cleveland, Craven, Haywood, and Robeson Counties. In fact, in his radio and television address on January 5, 1966, at the end of his first year in office, Governor Moore pointed out that four community colleges, two technical institutes, an industrial education center, and thirteen extension units were added to the system by the 1965 General Assembly. This was possible, in part, because the legislature had appropriated a record budget for the public school system of $528 million for the biennium, $106 million more than was spent in the previous two years. He stated, "Our programs for education beyond the high school have been broadened and are being made available to more and more citizens.... Now training is available to practically every citizen of our state at the forty-three institutions that make up the system."

The second year of the Moore administration, 1966, proved a record one for the new community college system in many ways, with developments that would prove critical for the system's future expansion and health. First, Dallas Herring and his supporters—by courting Edwin Gill, by developing the formula and promoting the system through the press and in-house publications—had won over Governor Moore. Tim Valentine, the governor's legal counsel, recalled, "Dan Moore had a lot of confidence in Mr. Gill, and I think Mr. Gill became indoctrinated with community college enthusiasm somewhere in the Moore years. And his office was in the capitol, right across from the governor's, and they visited back and forth. Edwin Gill was instrumental in interesting Moore in the system but as I recall he became a fervent adherent, and during his administration, the program was expanded."

Moore certainly wanted to commend the personnel of the system for their work while encouraging them to continue to focus on vocational training. On April 26 he invited the leaders of the system to Raleigh for a luncheon. Ben

Fountain recalled, "He invited all the presidents for a luncheon at the mansion—one of the few governors who ever did anything like that, I mean all of them. We had lunch at the mansion.... I can see him now standing there, where we were sitting around in the governor's mansion and talking to us in very positive manner and letting us know that he supported what we were doing."

The governor reminded the community college leaders that their institutions were uniquely equipped to meet the technical and vocational training needs of people who were beyond high school age. But he went on to say that this includes "removing those basic and high school level educational deficiencies of adults that keep them from succeeding in technical and vocational studies." Such thinking left the door open for other courses than just vocational and technical training in the colleges.

Chairman Herring certainly agreed with the governor's vision of a greater role for the community colleges. Speaking to the trustees of the North Carolina community colleges at a meeting in High Point on May 11, 1965, he echoed the governor's sentiments when he stated,

> Vocational and technical training, therefore, must remain the major emphasis of the community college system so long as these tremendous statewide needs exist. We cannot make the change to an industrial economy without this effort. There is no other place to which the people can turn for such training. But vocational and technical training alone will not be enough, for it is not machinery that we are changing and adapting for industrial production. Our students are human beings—not machines—and they have humanitarian needs as well as vocational and technical capabilities. Thousands of people in the state's workforce cannot even read and write the English language. Thousands have not graduated from high school. They cannot fit themselves for these new roles with this basic kind of education. Our task must include the correction of these deficiencies so long as they exist, and there must be no reduction in our effort here. The goal of the community college system must be as comprehensive as the needs of our students are. If this is not understood, then it is our duty to make it clear, so that

it will be understood. We must support policies which will open all of these doors to all of the people who can walk through them with any degree of promise to themselves and to the state.

The adult basic education (ABE) enrollments continued to increase exponentially in the colleges and technical institutes. In the second issue of *The Open Door*, published in the summer of 1965, Monroe C. Neff had predicted that by June of the next year, enrollments would more than double the 19,157 ABE students then in the program. By August 1966 the state board voted to approve receipts for ABE in the amount of $1,398,505 under the Economic Opportunity Act, representing 40,000 students enrolled in the ABE program. Tens of thousands were being taught to read and write, a critical role that would account for much of the growth of the colleges and make yet another strong argument for their expansion throughout the state.

Another event during the fall of 1966 would prove critical to the future leadership and staffing of the community college system. For some time, Chairman Herring had been concerned about the training and experience of community college personnel. In fact, some years back, Andy Jones, director of the Department of Administration during the Sanford years, had remarked to Herring that the community college system needed to have better-trained persons, especially deans and administrators, and that the Board of Education "needed to get a hold of that problem and create a program that would help." Realizing that the exponential growth of the system only amplified this need further, Herring approached the U.S. Department of Education in 1966 and secured a promise of $150,000 to help fund a program to train community college leaders. He decided to seek help in the university system. He approached administrators at both Chapel Hill and Charlotte and was turned down in both cases. Finally, that fall, Herring, accompanied by Monroe C. Neff and H. B. Monroe from the Department of Community Colleges, went to see Dr. Edgar Boone at North Carolina State. They asked him to design a program for the professional development of community college personnel, particularly presidents, deans, and other administrators. Boone agreed to do a proposal for an internship program that would provide promising students from the system with instruction and experiences that would allow them to go back into the system and provide "the kind of informed and well-trained management that the institutions desperately needed." Herring recalled later, "I tell you the truth, in fifteen minutes we agreed on it. He took it over, and it was one of the best decisions I have ever made in my life." The friendship and partnership formed that day would last well beyond the internship program it spawned and would greatly influence the new system.

It was estimated that at least 150 community college administrators in the state held master's degrees in various fields that would allow them to pursue advanced study leading to a doctoral degree in areas of administration, supervision, and curriculum development in adult education. In addition, over 300 deans, directors, and presidents could benefit greatly from in-service training. The five-year proposal that Boone submitted to the North Carolina State Board of Education was approved, with an operating budget of approximately $1 million. Over the course of the next five years, the department at N.C. State would confer 123 advanced degrees: 89 Master of Education, 16 Master of Science and 18 Doctor of Education degrees. Enrollment in the fall of 1968 had increased to slightly over 300. Herring later referred to the program as "one of the most fruitful investments of the tax dollar that I know of in education." The NCSU program borne of the Herring-Boone partnership would provide much of the leadership for the new system throughout the remainder of the twentieth century, and its impact is felt even today.

Enrollments in the community college system continued to soar. In the 1964–65 school year, the closing days of the Sanford administration, student enrollment in the system (unduplicated headcount) was 79,117. In his second *Year-End Report to the People*, which was broadcast by radio on December 30, 1966, Governor Moore reported that twenty-seven of the forty-three units in the community college system had building programs in progress to meet rapid enrollment increases. He went on to say that the system had also developed a stronger program for training the employees of new and expanding industries that year. Enrollment in the community college system was about 70 percent occupational, including training for sixty-nine industries. Ten percent of the students were in the college transfer program. Twenty percent were adults in elementary- and secondary-level (ABE) programs who never finished public school. Indeed, by the end of the 1965–66 school year, over 151,000 North

Carolinians had enrolled in the new institutions, an astounding increase of over 91 percent over the previous year.

In 1967 the population of North Carolina would surpass 5 million for the first time in the state's history. This statistic only served to underscore the importance of the community college system to the growing state. Education was to be the major emphasis for Governor Moore in his budget recommendation to the General Assembly that year. The public schools, the community college system, and higher education received about 73 cents of every general-fund dollar that the governor recommended. Indeed, by the time the General Assembly adjourned, technical institutes had been approved for seven more counties: Bladen, Edgecombe, Halifax, Martin, Montgomery, Nash, and Roanoke. The legislature had also appropriated over $43 million to expand the system, a 63 percent increase over the previous session. Six new extension units were to be opened, Wayne Technical Institute was to become a community college, and extension units in Craven and Beaufort Counties would become technical institutes. Indeed, with this expansion, 85 percent of North Carolina's high school graduates would now be within commuting distance of one of the system's forty-nine centers. The increase in enrollment was equally impressive that year. In the final spring quarter alone, about 80,000 students were enrolled in the community college system.

The years of the Moore administration saw not only the expansion of enrollments and institutions but also the beginning of an attempt to address the needs of those students interested in training for a four-year college degree. As Herring recalled, "We started bootlegging the liberal arts and sciences into the technical institutes and community colleges during the Moore administration." It began in the western part of the state, where travel could be especially difficult. Holland McSwain, who was president of Tri-County Tech, told Herring, "These mountain people are so far away from Western Carolina [University]." Herring responded, "They won't go to Western Carolina. Well, the thing for us to do is to take Western Carolina to them." Herring remembers that Governor Moore was at first uneasy with liberal arts in the technical institutes, but when assured of the need, he approved the addition. As Herring pointed out, "Hodges wouldn't agree to it, Sanford opened the door...but it was really Moore who said, 'Go ahead with it.'" Possibly the fact that Moore himself hailed from the region played a role in his decision. Nevertheless, at the June 1967 meeting, the State Board of Education for the first time approved a general education curriculum at Caldwell Technical Institute in Lenoir.

Also that summer, *The Open Door* reported that the Joint Committee on College Transfer Students, which had been meeting for over two years, was moving forward with plans to get colleges in North Carolina to accept community college students. Representing the North Carolina Association of Colleges and Universities, the State Board of Education, the State Board of Higher Education, and the North Carolina Association of Junior Colleges, the joint committee sought articulation agreements that would result in a commonly accepted program of general education in the first two years of study that would involve no loss of credits or time when a student transferred at the end of the sophomore year. Obstacles to the committee's success included quotas by five senior colleges and acceptance of only one year of work by two others. Regardless of the obstacles, students were beginning to see the community college system as a door to the senior colleges. For fall 1966 the five community colleges that were in full operation sent 148 transfer students to North Carolina's senior colleges and universities. By the fall of 1968, that number had increased to 629, an 85 percent increase over the previous year. Interestingly enough, in that year, the community colleges received 852 student transfers from the senior colleges and universities and private junior colleges (not counting those transferring into Central Piedmont Community College).

By the end of 1967 Governor Moore would report to the people of the state that the community college system had added a total of seven institutions that year, bringing the number of approved institutions to fifty. More than 166,000 people were taking advantage of the programs offered in the schools, and provisions were made for further expansion of the programs offered to include practical and registered nursing programs and numerous new occupational training programs. He stated, "There is opportunity within this system for any who will take advantage of it."

The growth of the Community College System continued apace until the end of the Moore administration. By September 1968 over 200,000 people were enrolled in the system, and forty-three institutions were in full operation. Speaking at the Manpower Conference in Raleigh called by Governor Moore in 1968, Dallas Herring reminded his audience of the importance and success of the community college movement. He pointed out that in the ten years since the first IEC opened its doors, over 309,000 jobs had been created in the state, 175,075 in new industry and 133,930 through the expansion of existing industry. Had the necessary occupational training not been provided, such a record of economic progress would have been impossible. From 1958 to 1968, over 318,000 individuals had received occupational training in the new institutions. This number did not take into account the thousands who benefited from the general education courses. It was a record of which Herring and Moore were justifiably proud.

By the end of his term the governor had become one of the strongest supporters of the Community College System, seeing its development as one of his administration's greatest achievements. He would state with pride,

> I cannot overemphasize the importance of the community college system to higher education. Tremendous progress had been made during my administration in expanding this system. There are now fifty technical institutes and community colleges in the system, one within commuting distance of about 90 percent of the people, but what is now being done through this system is only a sound beginning of what must be done in the years ahead. The "open door" policy is no longer enough. There must be a reaching out and recruiting effort made by the community college system, and programs must be broadened and developed to meet the needs of a progressive people and a growing state.

Moore's conservative nature may have kept him from mentioning one other fact. During his administration, appropriations for the community colleges had increased almost 400 percent.

Lieutenant Governor Bob Scott had decided that he would run for governor. A friend of community colleges, Scott faced J. Melville Broughton in the Democratic primary in 1968. Tall and dignified, Broughton represented the conservative wing of the Democratic Party, so naturally many of Dan Moore's people gravitated to him. On his left, Scott was opposed by Reginald Hawkins, a Charlotte dentist who was the first African American to seek the office of governor in North Carolina. Scott remembered,

> I had Melvin Broughton Jr., the son of a former governor, who was conservative and had the heritage of the conservative wing of the party. And on the right [left] we had the liberal Dr. Hawkins, Reginald Hawkins from Charlotte, who was a black dentist, well-spoken, impressive, good talker. And so I was in the middle of those two and I made it my campaign strategy to literally be in the middle and crowd the others over on the left and right shoulders of the road.

The strategy worked, and Scott went on to win the primary with 337,368 votes to Broughton's 233,924 and Hawkins's 129,808. Although Scott was about 26,000 votes short of a majority, Broughton wisely realized that he probably would not pick up enough of Hawkins's supporters to win. He chose not to ask for a second primary.

In the general election, Scott faced Rocky Mount businessman and one-term congressman James C. Gardner. A critical element in Scott's success was the support of Dan Moore. According to Scott, "Dan Moore supported me strongly. He raised money for me. He had dinners at the governor's mansion with businesspeople, asking them to support me and so on." Scott defeated Gardner by less than 100,000 votes: 821,000 to 737,000. At thirty-nine he became North Carolina's youngest elected governor in the twentieth century. And with his victory, community colleges had a proven friend in the governor's mansion who would ensure that the gains realized during the Moore administration would not only be permanent but would serve as a platform for greater expansion in the future.

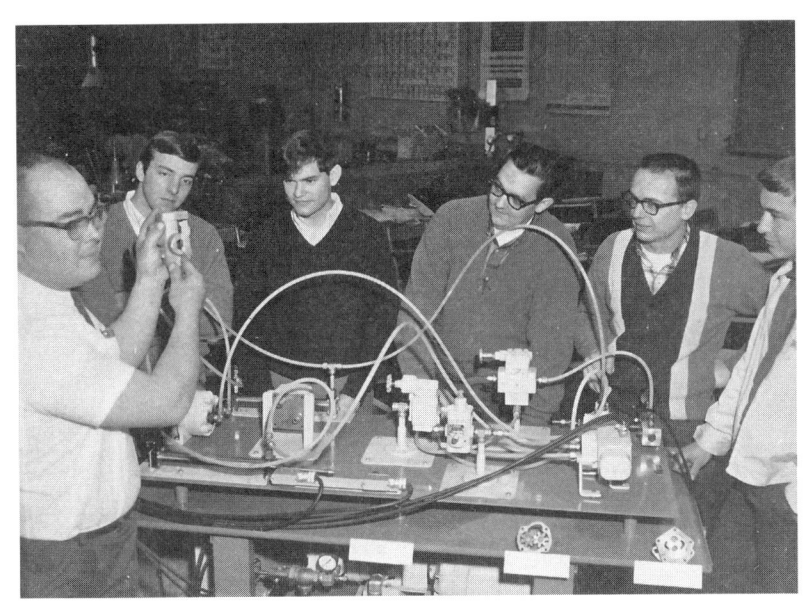

Students in a hydraulics class at Forsyth Technical Community College, 1967

Photography open house at Randolph Community College, 1968

Rowan-Cabarrus Community College drafting class, 1960s

First office tech program at Tri-County Community College in the late 1960s

V

Expansion
PLATEAU AND PROGRESS

Let the timid, the fainthearted, the foot-draggers, the "do-nothings" be forewarned. We are going to make progress in this administration. There is work to be done and we are going to get on with the job. In the tradition of others who have borne this great responsibility—Luther Hodges—Terry Sanford—Dan Moore—we too will point to the far plateau.
ROBERT SCOTT

We are convinced that we are doing a good job and we have the facts and figures to prove it, but as we progress from year to year, we must keep one salient point in mind—total education of all the people.
EPPS READY

The newly elected governor, Robert W. Scott, was no stranger to the North Carolina Community College System. Having served on the State Board of Education for the past four years as lieutenant governor, he had come to know members such as Dallas Herring and Barton Hayes, and shared their views on the value of the system to the state. Community colleges were to have his strong support while he was governor, and later he would serve as president of the system. However, during his administration he was concerned that the system not stray too far from its focus on workforce preparation. Even during the hard-fought election campaign in the fall of 1968, his opponent Jim Gardner had suggested, "We must reestablish our priorities in North Carolina as our vocational and industrial training is woefully inadequate to prepare our students for this technical age." Also at the time, G. L. Howard, director of new industry training in the Community College Department, left to take a similar position in Florida, but not before warning, "It is almost impossible for a man who is a community college president to wear both hats—academic and technical."

In view of these criticisms and others, it is not surprising that the issue was very much on Governor Scott's mind when he made his first speech to the North Carolina legislature on January 22, 1969. He stated, "In the technical institutes and community colleges, greater emphasis should be placed on vocational opportunities. Programs should be broadened in this area. They should be developed in coordination with occupational education in the public schools. And this training should be made more relevant to the economy of the state. The emphasis should be on the skills demanded by industry, especially the better-paying industrial and service jobs."

Scott had already noted that the fifty institutions "have grown rapidly," enrolling over 189,000 in 1969. He challenged the legislature when he said, "It is through these institutions that we can make a greater effort to reach more people—both adults and high school graduates."

Actually the community college system was already leading the way in vocational training. Since the first industrial education center had opened its doors ten years before, some 318,000 people had been trained to fill 309,005 new industrial jobs created across the state. That training was continuing, according to a 1968 federal report released in January. The federal government listed North Carolina as tied for third place among the states in percentage of employed workers enrolled in trade extension courses offered by the community college system and the public schools. In 1968 there were 34,480 students enrolled in those courses. In response to the criticism and the evidence of success, the State Board of Education reemphasized the role of the community colleges in industry training by adopting a new policy statement at its March meeting emphasizing that its desire to create more and better-paying jobs had been a major consideration in establishing the community college system. The policy stated that the Department of Community Colleges would work closely with the individual institutions to prepare legitimate training programs, tailor-made for each industry. However, regular curriculum and extension programs would remain oriented to the long-range and "broader educational needs of the student."

During the first two years of the Scott administration, the community college system continued its rapid growth. New programming included training geared to meet the needs of local governmental personnel, with courses such as Human Relations Training for Municipal Personnel and Supervisory Development Training for Public Works Department Laborers. Meanwhile, to encourage further development of general education programs, Director Epps Ready was given the power to approve the general education curriculum programs for all institutions in the community college system. Furthermore, the colleges also began awarding the associate in science degree to graduates in such preprofessional college transfer programs such as optometry, pharmacy, and veterinary medicine.

Institutions in the system not only continued to offer new programming but also began to enter into new partnerships with local municipalities and businesses. For example, Wayne Community College had begun offering instructional programs relating to air science occupations and technologies. This led to the Wayne County Airport asking the college to take over the airport's management. The result was that the county commissioners agreed to underwrite the college, and the college in turn managed the airport and integrated the management into its training program.

Four additional technical institutes were established in 1969—in Henderson, Johnston, Person, and Vance Counties. The technical institutes in Caldwell, Onslow, and Pitt Counties became community colleges. By the end of 1969, there were sixteen community colleges and thirty-eight technical institutes either operating or approved. The system now had an institution within commuting distance of almost 97 percent of the state's more than 5 million people. Governor Scott said, "This fine training program is going to the people. It is for them. It is their golden opportunity for meaningful and rewarding employment in the future."

The year 1970 would see the first formal marketing efforts directed at the general public. Plans were finalized to produce a fifteen-minute film depicting the system as a whole, from which color slides could be made for use by the

Department of Conservation and Development for attracting new industry. Other plans included a fifty-two-week series of fifteen-minute public service programs to be broadcast by radio, as well as packets of four or five thirty-second spot announcements emphasizing the economic advantages to be realized from an education, which would be distributed to radio and television stations at regular intervals. Finally, a series of programs concerning educational opportunities for women in the community college system was prepared by WRAL-TV along with several programs involving taped interviews with community college personnel.

In the east, exciting plans were afoot to make transferring to a senior college much easier for community college graduates. East Carolina's president, Leo Jenkins, met with the presidents of the system's forty-one community colleges and thirteen technical institutes. Jenkins called for agreements that would allow full acceptance as juniors at East Carolina University for any graduate from any institution within the community college system. Some presidents, including Robert LeMay of W. W. Holding Technical Institute of Raleigh, suggested that would either lower ECU's academic standards or change the vocational emphasis of the technical institutes, a continuing concern. In fact, the Advisory Budget Council, responding to concerns that the technical schools might have designs on becoming junior colleges and eventually regional universities, reissued Chapter 115-D of the Statement of Purpose in the community college law, which read, "The major purpose of each and every institution operating under the provisions of this Chapter shall be and shall continue to be the offering of vocational and technical education and training, and of basic, high school level, academic education needed in order to profit from vocational and technical education." Further, William Turner of the Department of Administration reminded colleges that vocational/technical funds should not be diverted for academic programs. He instructed that future budgets were to be prepared and presented in such a way that the amount of funds devoted to technical and vocational education and those for college-level training were to be shown separately.

The community college intern program at North Carolina State University continued to show tremendous progress and growth under the leadership of Dr. Edgar Boone. Indeed, by 1970 the program had awarded twenty-eight doctoral degrees and twenty-eight master's degrees, and fifteen doctoral degrees and twenty-eight master's degrees were due to be awarded within the next six months. In addition, seventy-two local staff members were currently pursuing degree programs, and over fifteen hundred administrators, faculty members, or staff had participated in conference activities or workshops. As stated in a spring 1969 edition of *The Open Door*, the intern program was providing graduate education, in-service education, as well as research and development for "North Carolina's burgeoning community college system." The newly renamed Department of Adult and Community College Education had become the major supplier of professional development and training for personnel within the system, and as such, it would continue to influence and mold the thinking of system leaders for many years to come.

The year 1970 not only witnessed further change but was a benchmark that saw the passing and retirement of two of the key leaders from the system's early years. First, A. Wade Martin died of a heart attack on October 20 at age fifty. Dallas Herring was very upset at the news of Martin's untimely passing and wrote in a letter to a friend, "No man so clearly left his mark on education in our region, or so soundly shaped its future course. I am deeply sorry to know that he is no longer with us, but I know that the spirit of what he stood for will last and will touch the lives of tens of thousands in a way no one else could." In closing, Herring challenged Martin's followers, "I know that you will do as he would want you to do—guard and protect the investment he made of his life by spreading his influence for good throughout the South in the new system of education he did so much to initiate."

On December 31, 1970, I. E. Ready retired as director of the Department of Community Colleges, a position he had held since 1963. Ready stated just prior to his retirement that "in his opinion, the biggest achievement of the community college–technical institute program to date is the tremendous acceptance of this program by the people of the state." Referring to the man whom Governor Scott once jovially referred to as the "daddy" of the system, Dallas Herring wrote, "The opportunity for total education is now a reality in North Carolina. The public schools, technical institutions, and community colleges are in reach of everyone.... No one has excelled Dr. I. E. Ready in patient understanding, in philosophical commitment, or in persistent dedication to the opening of these doors of new opportunity for the people of North Carolina." Herring went on to recall,

In thinking back to those early days when we began the curriculum study, the citizens' committee movement, and the industrial education centers, I am led to wonder just what would have happened if Dr. Ready had not come along at the right time with the right philosophy and the right temperament to help in these important and decisive events.... Those who write the history of these tumultuous times undoubtedly will conclude that the measures taken, which so much involved Dr. Ready's personal leadership, were pivotal and binding on the state's future in such a way that the schools were not only saved, but expanded and improved even as disaster threatened them.

Ready would not have much opportunity to use the new golf clubs presented to him by the North Carolina Occupational Directors' Association or to sit in front of the color TV given by the staff of the Department of Community Colleges, because upon retirement he became a professor in the Department of Adult and Community College Education at North Carolina State University. Ready would serve in that position for much of the next decade.

The community college system had changed greatly since it was formally established by the North Carolina legislature in 1963. All institutions that had been industrial education centers prior to that year had become either technical institutes or community colleges by 1970, and new institutions had been added. Fourteen institutions referred to themselves as colleges, thirty-nine used the term "institute" to describe themselves, and one—Caldwell Community College and Technical Institute—insisted that it was both. In Fiscal Year 1969–70, the full-time-equivalent enrollment in the system had increased to 47,836, an increase of 615 percent over the 7,781 recorded for FY 1963–64. Student enrollment had grown from 52,870 in 1963–64 to 293,602 in 1969–70, meaning nearly 6 percent of the state's population attended one of the system's institutions. Sixty-three percent of the students were able to attend local institutions in their own counties. Another 23 percent went to institutions in adjacent counties. Only 8.2 percent of in-state students had to travel farther, and only 2.7 percent were from out of state.

The demographics of the student population had also changed significantly. In 1963 the great majority of students were white, male, and enrolled in occupational/vocational education. By 1969–70, minority (nonwhite) enrollment was 21.9 percent, over 60,000 students. Female students accounted for almost half of the student population, 49.2 percent. Of the total student population, 2,171 transferred to in-state senior colleges and universities, 25 percent of those to private institutions. (Despite the concerns of some about the college transfer function increasing at the expense of vocational technical training, less than 5 percent of the total student population was enrolled in the college transfer program in 1970.)

To bring about this expansion of education in North Carolina, the state and federal governments had invested (along with student tuition fees) a total of $36,251,294 in 1969–70, up from just over $4 million ($4,074,962) in 1963–64. (The state could be justly proud of this major investment, viewed in the context of the original $500,000 appropriation voted for the industrial education center program in 1957.) At the local level, expenditures had increased during the Ready years from $603,898 to $4,789,639, an increase of 793 percent, and strong evidence supporting Ready's statement that the people firmly believed in and supported their local community colleges.

Equipment and book costs had increased as well. As of June 30, 1970, major equipment totaled $18,467,928 systemwide, of which 71 percent was in occupational education equipment and 24 percent in general administrative equipment. Two percent was for adult education equipment and only 3 percent for college transfer. Books, tallied separately, had a valuation of $3,523,940 systemwide at an estimated cost of $8.50 per book. By 1970, there were approximately seven books for each student in the system.

During those early years, the curriculum had expanded dramatically as well. As mentioned earlier, when the community college system came into existence, there were only 8 occupational areas in the curriculum. By 1969–70, that number had reached 150 separate areas of occupational study. They included areas such as health occupations, engineering technologies, welding, data processing, auto mechanics, marine technology, and art and design. In 1970, new programs were still being added. A course in technical illustrating was offered at the Technical Institute of Alamance, recreation technology at Southwestern Technical Institute, and hospital plant maintenance at McDowell Technical Institute. Other new programs started in 1970 included a program in inhalation therapy, which grew out of an educational partnership formed by Durham Technical Institute and Duke University Medical Center. In that program, students took their academic courses at the technical institute while the clinical sessions were held across town at the medical center. Durham Tech also began a new program in opticianry, which was planned in conjunction with leading opticians, ophthalmologists, optometrists, and educators. The *Gastonia Gazette* discussed the change in the curricula, highlighting environmental engineering courses at Fayetteville Technical Institute, and predicted that colleges in the 1970s must be prepared to "accept women in educational programs that were once considered in a man's domain."

As Herring and Ready suggested, the 1960s did see the dream of an open door to education and opportunity become a reality for the people of North Carolina—so much so that when Bob Scott gave his "Year End Report to the People of North Carolina," he, too, would point to an enrollment in the community college system of 295,000, which reflected a 22 percent increase over the previous academic year. Further, in 1970 the Person Technical Institute had opened its doors, and Caldwell and Onslow Technical Institutes had become community colleges. Fourteen of the fifty-four institutions in the community college system had completed major capital improvements during the year, and sixteen others had initiated such capital projects. Scott stated with pride, "During the year a federal official who works with junior colleges across the country stated that North Carolina's system of community colleges and technical institutes ranks among the top five in the nation." With well over 95 percent living within commuting distance of a community college or technical institute, the impractical dream of access for all to higher education, which had been a vision for some, had become a reality for most people in North Carolina.

At the January 7, 1971, State Board of Education meeting in Raleigh, Dr. Ben E. Fountain had assumed the position of state director in a smooth transition that the board had announced at its September meeting. Fountain had been handpicked by Herring and enjoyed the support of the overwhelming majority of the board. He had been a superintendent of public schools prior to becoming the president of what became Lenoir Community College. While there he caught the eye of Herring and so came to Raleigh in 1971 to take the helm of the system. Fountain remembered, "In retrospect, it would have been better for me personally to have gone to Raleigh in July ... coming into Raleigh simultaneously with the legislature, I didn't have time to turn around before I was over there working in the General Assembly. And my scope was fairly limited in knowledge of the whole system. Took me two years to get around to visiting all the schools." It is little wonder in view of the rapid growth and challenges facing the system in these last years of the Scott administration.

During 1971–72, enrollment in the community college system's fifty-six institutions had increased to 358,000, and vocational and technical programs numbered over 170. Appropriations to the community college system had increased more than 135 percent during the preceding four years. Fears that the community colleges would become four-year institutions had proved to be unfounded. As Governor Scott pointed out in a speech to the Joint Conference of North Carolina Industrial Developers Association and North Carolina Association of Public Community College Presidents in Fayetteville in February 1972, "Since 1963, when the system was established, not a single community college or technical institute has become a four-year school," and less than 5 percent of the system's total enrollment was in college-parallel work. Scott would go on to encourage the industrial developers and the community college leaders to lay "a framework for even greater economic and educational opportunities for this generation of North Carolinians and those to follow." The community colleges would continue to play a key role in that partnership, not only through its curricular vocational and technical training, but through the industrial training program housed in the Department of Community Colleges and Technical Institutes. The program was the oldest in the Southeast and was hailed by Scott in a later trip he made to Tokyo in the fall of 1972.

By that time, North Carolina was facing great change not just in its economic and social landscape but politically, which some feared might result in retrenchment. As Governor Scott looked ahead in late 1972, he predicted that the next governor "will be able to meet the needs for new and expanded services of essential programs and, if he chooses, recommend measures of tax relief." One of the areas he pointed out that should be expanded and strengthened, even as tax relief was provided, was the community college system. Surprisingly enough, that responsibility of fulfilling that twin challenge would fall to a young Republican swept into office by the Nixon landslide, James E. Holshouser.

Benjamin E. Fountain Jr., 1971–1978

Commercial fishing program at Cape Fear Community College

Counseling Vietnam veterans at Richmond Community College campus, 1976

EXPANSION: PLATEAU AND PROGRESS 97

Graduates of the EMT program at Davidson County Community College, 1974

Men's basketball team at Gaston College, 1972

Automotive class conducted at Sandhills Community College, 1972

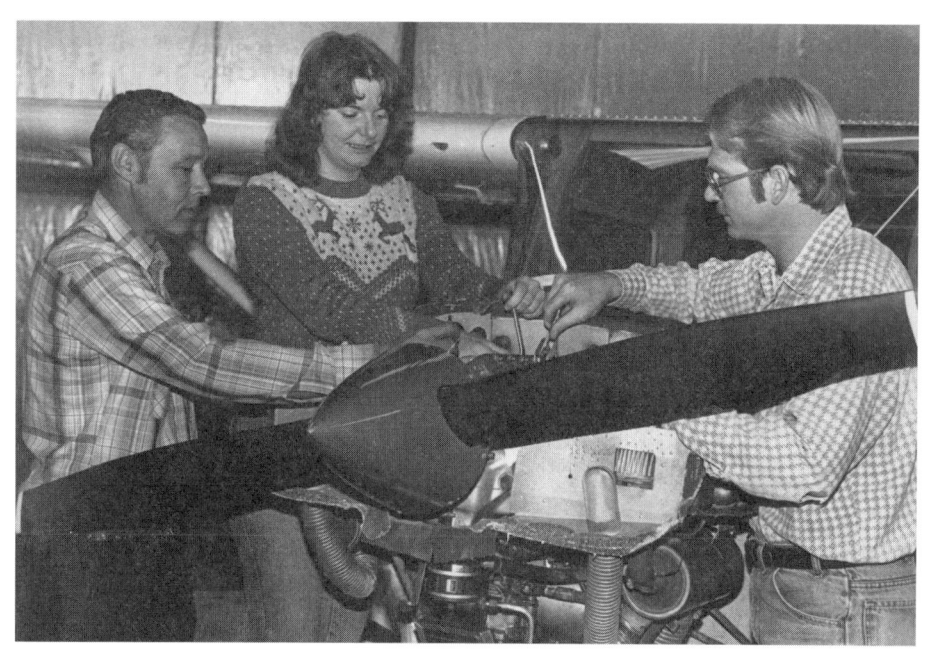

Aviation systems technology class at Wayne Community College

VI

Renaissance and Reformation

Jim Hunt was lieutenant governor under Jim Holshouser and Jim Hunt was very helpful during those years. As a matter of fact, Holshouser agreed to break the $500,000 limit on capital funds for the community college system and Hunt did too. So they both agreed together. And Holshouser got us some extra, we had had kind of a dry spell for appropriations and Holshouser helped.

BEN FOUNTAIN

For we strike out on a bold new trail—with new ideas, new methods—yes a new vision for our state.... So let us declare that quality education will be the polar star which will guide us toward a future of promise.

JIM HOLSHOUSER

Many people have voiced many good ideas about what community colleges need to do, but the main goal has always been and still remains the same: to make a better life for the people of North Carolina.

JIM HUNT

In his inaugural address, Jim Holshouser declared, "Quality education will be the polar star that will guide us toward a future of promise." The new governor was no stranger to what quality education could mean in life. Born in Boone during the height of the Great Depression, he attended Appalachian High School. After graduation, Holshouser enrolled in Davidson College and then attended law school at the University of North Carolina at Chapel Hill, where he was inducted into Phi Alpha Delta law fraternity before graduating in 1960. Returning to Boone, the young attorney quickly became involved in politics and was elected to the legislature in 1962. He would remain a member of the General Assembly until he became the first Republican governor to be elected in the Tar Heel state in the twentieth century. But though conservative in the eyes of many, he understood both the promise and importance of education. And to the surprise of some, he refused to go back on the promises of earlier administrations to provide adequate resources to public education, particularly to the community colleges.

Speaking to assembled thousands on the east grounds of the capitol on a cold January day in 1973, Holshouser declared, "Our future must hold more than highways. In fact, when we build for the future we know that the cornerstone will bear the name, 'Education.'" Less than two weeks later, Holshouser surprised many by actually recommending increases in spending on education, particularly for community colleges. In his budget message to the General Assembly, he spelled out an ambitious expansion plan, supporting the commitments of former governor Bob Scott. He stated, "I endorse the recommendation of the Advisory Budget Commission, for a $29 million increase in operating funds for the community college system." He went on to propose an additional $15.1 million in capital funds to honor the state's original commitment in 1963 for capital funds to each institution. To ensure that the community remained committed as well, he urged retention of the policy requiring that any additional funds beyond this original amount would have to be raised locally. Ultimately the General Assembly would provide an appropriation of $25 million.

February 1973 brought further changes in state leadership that would impact the future of the community colleges. In that month James B. Hunt Jr., the new lieutenant governor, began meeting with the State Board of Education. At that same meeting, the state board, chaired by Dr. Dallas Herring, acted upon the request from a delegation in Iredell County for the establishment of a comprehensive institution in Statesville, which involved an acceptance of Mitchell College into the system, subject to the favorable action of the General Assembly. This would be the fifty-seventh local institution to join the system since its birth. In fact, in a brief report to the board the previous month, Dr. Raymond Stone, president of Sandhills Community College, had pointed out that as of 1972, the system encompassed fifty-six institutions, fifteen community colleges and forty-one technical institutes.

With the generous support of the General Assembly and the visionary leadership of men like Herring and Holshouser, that growth would continue. In his second Legislative and Budget Message to the General Assembly, in January 1974, Governor Holshouser again called for a record expenditure of funds. In fact, the recommendation of the Advisory Budget Commission, which was endorsed by Holshouser, was $2,995,172,039, the largest one-year state budget proposal in the history of North Carolina. In his speech to the General Assembly, Holshouser stated, "Our contributions to public education did not stop at the high school level. The tremendous boost given our community college system was the first major change in meeting that system's capital needs since it was established in 1963." Holshouser went on to recognize the increasing role that the community colleges played in the North Carolina educational system by recommending another $10 million in capital funds for the colleges. However, funding for operating costs within the Advisory Budget Commission feel short of needs due to the system's rapid growth. Later that spring, system president Ben Fountain would warn that funding the system at the amount before the General Assembly would force the closing of the open door; for the first time, some institutions would have to turn away students. Fountain stated that the system could not handle the students "we have now," pointing out that enrollments just in the prior year had increased from 59,000 in the fall of 1973 to 72,000 in the fall of 1974. In fact, over 400,000 students had attended the seventeen community colleges and forty technical institutes in that time, approximately 79,500 full-time equivalents. He warned that enrollment projections put the system's student population in the coming year at nearly 107,000 FTE. If that materialized without significant funding increases, only 88 percent of expected applicants in fall 1975 would be admitted.

In addition to a shortage of funds and increasing enrollments, the system was wrestling with concerns over a shortage of African American leadership and increasing unease with the state board leadership. During the summer of 1975,

Dr. Prezell Robinson was joined by E. H. Oxendine and Mildred Strickland in expressing concern at the lack of diversity among presidents of the local institutions. In fact, in a statement he read into the minutes of the May meeting, Dr. Robinson stated his disappointment that a black president wasn't chosen for Durham Technical Institute. He said, "Now in my judgment, Durham Technical Institute is a prime example of where a minority person qualified could do and fill a top post. I believe the representation in Durham Technical Institute is above 60 percent minority in terms of this student body." Dr. Robinson went on to express his hope that, though he knew the state board could not dictate whom the local board hired, "It is my sincere conviction if this board feels strongly enough, it can exert a degree of influence, not coercion, but it can exert moral influence that I think will have a salutary effect on local boards." It would be many years before his hope of greater diversity would become reality, but the day would come.

In the interim, state board chairman Dallas Herring reminded a state in the throes of economic recession and social unrest, "It is probably true that no other state, north or south, has more fully complied with the constitutional mandate for equal opportunity in education than North Carolina has. The idea of quality in education is more complex.... Full and free discussions ought to be encouraged, for it is the only way to arrive at a democratic decision about public policy in education." Herring was echoing thoughts expressed by Governor Holshouser some months earlier when he challenged community college leaders at a conference in Raleigh "to strive for greater excellence in all of our programs, our offerings. I don't mean that we simply must have an abundant quantity of instruction. We also must have an abundance of quality of excellence in our instruction." Holshouser suggested that community colleges would be held accountable, as all levels of education would, to show that tax dollars were spent wisely. He went on to recommend that, in addition to looking at management by objective, community college leaders should consider incentive formula budgeting. Both he and Herring realized that in the future the General Assembly would be concerned with the return on its investment.

Some in the General Assembly were already concerned about the future of the system—including a growing sentiment that there should be a separate policy board for the community college system. In the summer of 1975 a draft bill calling for a separate board was being circulated and discussed by members of the Senate Education Committee, and its backers were calling for a study commission. Chairman Herring and system president Fountain both took a dim view of the idea. They were joined by the editors of the *News and Observer*, who wrote in June that the mission of the community college system is much more like that of the public schools than it is different. They concluded that the fifty-seven technical institutes and community colleges had fared well under the leadership of the State Board of Education and system president Ben Fountain. Furthermore, they opined that it was doubtful that the Democratic legislature would extend new appointive powers to a sitting Republican governor.

Later that year, the state board issued a policy statement strongly opposing the idea of a separate board for community colleges. It consisted of four pages of rationale and concluded, "For these and other important reasons, we oppose any effort to remove the community college system from the jurisdiction of this board, which initiated the system in the first place and which carefully governed its growth alongside the public school ever since." The statement heralded the mutual support and cooperation of the public schools and community colleges, pointing out that this cooperation had been critical to the economic advances of the past decade. In fact, the resolution pointed to the reversal of the trend of outmigration of the state's population and the increasing of the number of manufacturing jobs from 470,000 to 814,000 since 1957.

The political pressure from the General Assembly along with a report produced by the Research Triangle Institute would result in an important new commission on the future of the community college system. The report, titled "Development of North Carolina Community College Planning Capabilities," was prepared by Stephen Johnston and Hazel R. Jolley. Terrance Tollefson, vice president for planning and coordination, and Marcus Allred provided guidance to the project. The report maintained that if enough money and facilities were made available, the system could more than double its enrollments to 1.1 million students by 1980–81. It detailed the need to plan more effectively for the future and the potential that existed for the community college system's involvement in "providing educational services to the North Carolina workforce and general population, based primarily on manpower requirements in state and substate regional economies." The report's recognition of the need for more effective planning tracked well with both Governor Holshouser's concern over the need for greater quality and Lieutenant Governor Jim Hunt's suggestion in a speech in Winston-Salem of the need for a study commission. The board proceeded to establish its own committee to develop a blueprint for the future of the community college system. In its final meeting in 1975 the board recognized that "whereas, a new examination of the system's role in the total educational picture for approximately the next 20 years is now desirable and necessary... therefore, be it resolved that the chairman of the State Board of Education appoint a committee to develop a blueprint for the future of the community college system to be recommended to the State Board of Education." Dr. Edgar J. Boone, head of the Department of Adult and Community College Education at North Carolina State University, was appointed chairman of the Commission on the Future of the North Carolina Community College System. The thirty-one-member panel would spend the next year overseeing a study of the system, developing a strategic plan and working to produce its report.

The next two years would be particularly challenging ones for the community college system in the areas of leadership and funding. The continuing recession resulted in a $4.2 million operating budget reduction by the General Assembly at the same time system enrollment was up 30 percent. The limited budget strained the ability of the colleges to address the needs of the increasing number of students as well as the continual calls for increasing the quality of education at the colleges. As Chairman Herring stated to the Community College and Vocational Committee at the February 1976 state board meeting, "If the service for which the students paid cannot be rendered without reduction in quality, it seems to me the money should be returned.... We make no complaint about the budget reduction or about the fact that the state is unable to provide its usual share of funding for these unexpected students." But President Ben Fountain warned that the budget restrictions could result in overloaded teachers, dropped courses, and students turned away from classes. Yet despite the reductions, community colleges continued to provide the necessary training for students to secure new or better jobs. In March 1976, in addition to the degrees awarded at the system's community colleges, there were 113 approved technical programs (22 new ones) and 88 vocational programs.

A concern with quality education would also lead to a dramatic change in system leadership in the closing days of the Holshouser administration. Some years back, Herring became concerned over state superintendent A. Craig Phillips's move to diversify the cadre of teachers in North Carolina by reducing requirements surrounding the administration of the National Teaching Exam. This basic disagreement on direction was further exacerbated when concerns surfaced that Phillips's Department of Public Instruction "had juggled statistics to improve a report on the state kindergarten program." By the spring of 1976, the split had escalated to the point that Herring's supporters recruited Ben F. Currin, superintendent of the Rocky Mount Schools, to run against Phillips in the Democratic primary. Phillips's side, with some success, spread the rumor that the continued disputes were not over educational quality but issues concerning the community colleges and technical institutes. Jim Hunt, in the race for governor, linked the growth of the system with his own record as lieutenant governor, citing expanding enrollments, increasing programs in adult basic education, new equipment and curricula, and $35 million in capital improvements. However, when other candidates came out in support of a separate board, Hunt refused to take a position.

Meanwhile, community colleges saw and seized the opportunity to expand their offerings and student population by partnering with the military in North Carolina. In August 1976 the board instructed the department to develop a policy that would enable institutions to serve the military and other similar federal/state agencies without duplication of effort. The institutions involved included Fayetteville Technical Institute, Pitt Technical Institute, Central Carolina Technical Institute, and Pamlico Technical Institute. A letter from Swanson Richards, president of the North Carolina Association of Public Community College Presidents, to J. D. Porter, State Board of Education system controller, said that the colleges unanimously supported classes being held at military bases. In February 1977 the board supported the presidents' recommendation to include the specification that the home institution (main campus) would be responsible for educational classes at military installations.

The system also expanded its efforts to revitalize and support education and development in rural areas using the latest technology. Funds totaling $77,376 from the adult basic education and vocational education research areas were authorized for the first phase of the North Carolina Rural Renaissance Project. The monies were to support a consortium of ten technical institutes and community colleges, headed by Central Piedmont Community College, to develop audiovisual instructional materials to beam educational and health materials to rural areas of the state utilizing television broadcasts. More traditional methods of learning also expanded as sometime during the month of December, the state system reported over 1 million books in its learning resource centers. And it was also announced that by year's end, over $214,164,908 had been spent on capital expenditures since the department began in 1963.

The new year, 1977, saw far-reaching changes in the community colleges in North Carolina. On January 8, a new governor, James Baxter Hunt Jr., was inaugurated, and he was no stranger to education or the community colleges. His inaugural address gave no clue as to his plans for the system, beyond his concluding statement, "Let us commit ourselves—here today—to a new beginning for North Carolina." But as a member of the Board of Education, he had been at the center of the controversy surrounding the future of education that swirled around Herring and Phillips. And in his State of the State address, delivered to the General Assembly a week later on January 15, Hunt requested more money for community colleges, over $6 million to support a more liberal funding formula. In addition he challenged community colleges to "do a far better job of teaching our people the skills they will need to hold the good jobs of the 1980s." He provided more money in his budget to support that change.

Even as the state board considered the budget for the coming year, it did so in the light of year-end reports showing that after a decade of booming expansion, student enrollments were in a state of decline. The *News and Observer* reported that the 1975–76 FTE count of 102,451 was expected to drop to 97,000 for 1976–77. The leadership of the General Assembly, particularly the Senate Ways and Means Committee and the House Appropriations Committee, agreed with the governor that there needed to be a major review of how the system was funded.

In March of that year, the thirty-one-member Commission on the Future of the System, chaired by Dr. Ed Boone, presented its report to the State Board of Education. The commission report, in line with economic and political realities, as well as educational needs, called for a shift in emphasis from system expansion to the enhancement of quality in programming and efficiency in delivery of instruction and training. Furthermore, the report, in contradiction of a recent legislative report by Senator Ed Renfrow's commission, supported the continuing jurisdiction of the State Board of Education over the Department of Community Colleges. The new governor, however, had other plans.

Governor Hunt had changed his mind on the need for a separate board for the community colleges and, in addition, had made the difficult decision to not reappoint Dallas Herring to the State Board of Education. Craig Phillips had won reelection as state superintendent, and as Hunt recalled later, referring to the joint roles of the superintendent and board chair, "It was constitutional, and you couldn't change it by law. And the superintendent and the state board chairman just had to work together.... But by the way, nobody's ever respected and appreciated Dallas any more than I have." In fact, two years later, in a speech given at a dinner in Herring's honor, Hunt would state, "We have all heard of 'education governors'—from Charles Brantley Aycock to Terry Sanford. Notwithstanding all their accomplishments, I don't believe any individual has meant more to education in North Carolina than Dr. Dallas Herring."

Change came swiftly to the board. In March, Hunt called Herring to Raleigh and told him he would not be reappointed. Herring submitted his resignation to the board that month, and his supporters on the board proceeded to elect Lieutenant Governor Jimmy Green as chairman to serve out Herring's term, which ended April 30. Green's time as chairman was short-lived, however, as in May the board elected Dr. H. David Bruton, a pediatrician from Southern Pines, as chair of the State Board of Education. As Dallas Herring had served on the board for twenty-two years, twenty years as its chairman, it was truly the end of an era. In an attempt to begin the process of reconciliation of the board's factions, Chairman Bruton's first order of business was to name a committee, chaired by Herring friend and supporter R. Barton Hayes, to seek suitable means to recognize and honor Dallas Herring's service to the State Board of Education and to North Carolina.

Less than a week after the May 5 meeting, state senator Robert W. Wynne Jr. of Wake County introduced a bill to create a State Board of Community Colleges and Technical Institutes, which he believed would allow the state to exercise greater control over both spending and policy within the community college system. During this time, President Robert LeMay of Wake Technical Institute, whose school was facing scrutiny in the press for questionable fiscal practices, called for a two-thirds reduction in Department of Community College System staff along with a separate board. Others, such as board member John Tart, accused politicians of manipulating the system for their own political gain. Governor Hunt urged the state to exert stronger control over the system's fiscal activities, but stopped short of publicly endorsing the new board. Meanwhile, state president Ben Fountain stated, "I have studied the issue since 1965. My own personal and professional judgment has been and is consistently that the students and the education system in the state are well served with the present governing arrangement." However, the critical status of system funding would divert attention away from the question of governance.

As the new State Board of Education reorganized under Bruton that summer, it became painfully obvious that the system was underfunded. For a while in early June, local presidents faced the prospect of operating with $7.4 million, which was only 70 percent of their needed expenses. Though the Department of Administration finally authorized an additional $3.9 million of the $11.6 million needed, the crisis underscored the need for a new look at system funding. In fact, in July, many local institutions faced their worst financial crisis in years. State president Fountain responded by asking the board to allow colleges to use funds earmarked for new equipment to pay core faculty and staff and avoid mass furloughs and potential losses.

Throughout the remainder of the year, community colleges wrestled with budget shortages. Board chairman Bruton, in an address to community college presidents in Wilmington in early August, stated, "We must end this insane full-time equivalent student hours chase and constant expansion and contraction of our faculties." In hopes of finding the solution, he announced the reactivation of the Community College Advisory Council, whose twenty members would include Dr. Edgar J. Boone, chair of the Department of Adult and Community College Education at N.C. State; Billy Mills, a member of the University Board of Governors; and state senator Edward Renfrow. But budget cutbacks continued. Dr. Gerald James, president of Rockingham Community College, wrote to Hugh Battle, associate vice president of institutional services at the Department of Community Colleges, that there was a real concern about quality of the college offerings, given the reductions that colleges had made. He wrote, "The effect is being felt in the quality of work we are able to accomplish.... We need some relief." He concluded that the possibility of a callback of funds had caused a festering morale problem that could pose to be more damaging than the actual reduction in funds. Other presidents echoed his concern, including President Robert E. Paap of Catawba Technical Institute, who stated, "This shortsightedness of our funding system, the General Assembly, and the governor should not be taken out on them [community college personnel]." To forestall the cuts in pay for personnel, some local leaders, such as Gaston County commissioners, stepped in and helped their community colleges weather the budget cuts.

Meanwhile, rumors of further leadership changes swirled around the state capital. At year's end, the *News and Observer* reported that some state board members, among them Lieutenant Governor Jimmy Green, R. Barton Hayes, and Evelyn S. Tyler, were seeking to replace President Fountain. Seeking to shore up support for the embattled president, both Jeff Hockaday, chairman of the North Carolina Association of Community College Presidents, and Governor Hunt expressed their appreciation for the "good job" that Fountain had done. Finally, at its first meeting in 1978, the board voted to "affirm its position of having no immediate plans to alter the current state leadership" of the system.

Fountain announced in January that he was requesting the controller's office to adopt the Advisory Council's proposal on how to count student enrollment. The result would be that the 1978–79 budget adjustment request for the system would total $153,548,698 for the total operating budget, $13,497,207 for equipment and library books, and $9,243,200 for capital improvements. Interestingly enough, since 1963, over $229 million had been expended or obligated. The state had contributed 22 percent, the federal government had given 27 percent, but over 50 percent had been contributed by local government. In March and April the state board moved forward on the new community college funding formula and sent to the General Assembly a policy statement in reference to it, along with the Administrative Procedures Rules necessary for implementation of the formula.

Even though Chairman Bruton had reaffirmed in May that President Fountain was no longer under any pressure to leave his position, Fountain announced at the June meeting that he would assume the presidency of Isothermal Community College in Spindale upon Dr. Fred Eason's retirement in August. The board proceeded to adopt unanimously a resolution in Fountain's honor that read in part, "During his tenure as President he has seen the inadequate and makeshift facilities on most of our campuses replaced by modern buildings... to better meet the demands of the increasing thousands in North Carolina who are waiting to walk through the 'Open Door' to a new world of personal fulfillment." Indeed, prior to his departure at the next board meeting in July, the board received a request from the Brunswick County Board of Commissioners asking that the State Department of Community Colleges consider locating a technical institute in Brunswick County. Its eventual approval by the legislature the following year would bring the System to fifty-eight local community colleges and technical institutes. Also, in July, Richard Manz, chair of the Community Colleges Committee of the State Board and vice chair of the state board, announced that Charles R. Holloman would take charge of the department until a new president was named. As such, he would serve as senior vice president in charge for almost a year, as the state board sought to replace Fountain.

Throughout Holloman's tenure, the system wrestled with continuing funding constraints and attempts to diversify faculty, staff, and students. In September, an annual report titled "The Revised North Carolina State Plan for the Further Elimination of Racial Duality in the Public Higher Education Systems, Phase II: 1978–83" was presented to the board. It sought to disestablish the structure of the dual system and desegregate faculty, administrative staffs, nonacademic personnel, and governing boards. Some, including board member John Tart, had maintained that the system had never "practiced racial discrimination in services or employment" in either its history or its philosophy. Regardless, the system continued to focus on the issue, and in December the department's Division of Planning and Policy presented the board with a plan titled "Upgrading Minorities: Patterns and Trends, 1970 to 1978."

The new year saw not only a new system president but a new way of referring to the colleges within the system. Neither occurred, however, without serious opposition, and in the case of the naming of the president, serious political infighting occurred. At the first meeting in January, the Community College Advisory Council urged the board to consider changing the names of all institutions so that, no later than January 1, 1980, institutions within the system operating as community colleges would include the term "community college" in their name and technical institutes would include in their name the term "technical college." Local boards could, by a two-thirds majority vote, retain their existing name. The change was seen as necessary to add prestige to the campuses as well as making it easier for them to secure federal aid. Some did not share that vision. Regardless, in May 9, the state legislature passed the bill providing for the change.

By January, the presidential search committee was winding down its work. The three finalists were former governor Robert Scott; Dr. Larry J. Blake of Fraser Valley College in Chilliwack, British Columbia; and Dr. Eugene Speller, an African American community college president from Chicago. Even as support for Blake grew, support for Scott was expressed by several legislators, and twenty-six out of fifty state senators introduced a resolution urging "state agencies to hire North Carolinians for top state posts." Even former governor Jim Holshouser joined in lobbying for the resolution backing Scott. Other supporters included state senators Harold Hardison of Lenoir and W. Craig Lawing of Mecklenburg and the presiding officer of the senate, Lieutenant Governor Jimmy Green. However, Governor Jim Hunt opposed Scott's selection. Though he had told Scott and his uncle, powerful state senator Ralph Scott, that he was not opposed to Scott seeking the job, many Hunt administration officials were concerned about a former governor in a state post in which he might become a rival. Though Hunt made it clear that he was not going to be involved, stating, "I have great respect for both the board and the committee, and it's their decision to make," several on the board had been appointed by Hunt. On January 30 the state board met in executive session to hear the report of the search committee, just hours after the state senate passed the "Scott" resolution by a 43-3 vote. Two days later, ignoring the potential political fallout, the state board met in full session and named Dr. Larry Blake president in a 10-2 vote, with one abstention. The reaction in the senate was swift, with Senator J. J. "Monk" Harrington of Bertie summing up feelings there by stating, "It just burns me to a crisp." His appointment in the face of such vocal opposition, along with the 26 percent increase in the president's salary to match his former salary in Canada that was approved in February, did not set well with many North Carolinians and their representatives. Though he enjoyed the support of the state board and the governor, difficult days were ahead for Blake.

In May 1979 Governor Hunt, while speaking to the North Carolina Trustees Association of Community College Institutions, publicly threw his support behind the creation of a separate governing board. He stated, "I am today urging the General Assembly to enact legislation creating a separate, independent state policy-making board with jurisdiction over our network of community colleges and technical institutes. I believe that the general approach set out in the bill sponsored by Senator Billy Mills is a good one." Hunt went on to say that this step was needed in view of the new presidency of Larry Blake, to give him the best tools to assure his success. In addition, the governor felt that a separate state board could devote its attention and energies to making sure the community college system was doing a better job of educating and training North Carolinians in the higher skills required by new and expanding industries. He pointed to the fact that the state had already attracted about $1.3 billion in planned industrial development in 1979, and hoped to match the almost $2 billion achieved in 1978. The system needed to stand ready to meet the training needs that this new industry generated.

With the governor's support, the Mills bill, known as "An Act to Revise the Provisions Relating to the Administration of the Community Colleges and Technical Institutes," began to gain real support in the legislature. A similar bill in the House was introduced by Representative Bertha Holt of Alamance. Though the State Board of Education remained opposed to the idea, even passing unanimously a resolution opposing the now renamed Mills-Holt bill in May, the Trustees Association strongly supported it as they feared an erosion of local autonomy in competing ideas of governance, such as moving the community colleges under the University's Board of Governors. The Mills-Holt bill provided for a planning committee to be created in July, followed by a report from that committee in early 1980, and then the new seventeen-member board would assume control in January 1981. Eight members would be appointed by the governor and seven by the legislature, with the lieutenant governor and state treasurer serving ex officio. Vice President in Charge Holloman warned, pointing to the major shift of authority to local trustees, that "the state cannot afford a union in which all the members seceded.... It would cease to be a system." Though opposed by Holloman, the state board, and even former governor Bob Scott, the Mills-Holt bill became law on June 7, and the system would now come under the authority of a newly constituted nineteen-member Board of Community Colleges and Technical Institutes.

In addition to a new governing board, another milestone occurred in the summer of 1979. On May 1, upon a motion by John A. Pritchett and seconded by Dr. John A. Tart, Dr. Neill McLeod was approved as president of Martin Community College, effective May 14. Dr. McLeod was the first woman to serve as a community college president in North Carolina. Dr. Prezell Robinson again reminded the board that there was no minority president serving and urged that the next president appointed be of a "minority race." The entire board congratulated Dr. McLeod on her singular accomplishment.

On July 7 Dr. Larry Blake assumed the office of the president of the System of Community Colleges and Technical Institutes. He stated that one of the major questions that had to be answered during the eighteen-month transition period from one governing board to another related to the appropriate role of the Department of Community Colleges. "Where do you draw the line on when the state department makes a decision and when the local boards decide?" Questions such as this would have to be dealt with and determined during the transition period. Former governor Terry Sanford served as chairman of the thirteen-member planning commission, which was tasked by the legislature to recommend an orderly transition plan. Governor Hunt reminded the commission, "We have just got to do a better job of vocational training if we are to attract industry." In the coming months, the state's industrial recruiters were directed to work more closely with the system to see that the better training was provided so as to deliver the skilled workforce needed. The *News and Observer* noted that "if the state is to shed its low-wage status, the community college system must reassert its critical role in skills training." As such, it seemed that both Blake and the *N&O* wanted to refocus the system on job training and away from general education and college transfer.

President Blake proceeded with his plans to reorganize the Department of Community Colleges so that it would provide master planning for the system; seek to acquire necessary funding to fulfill its mission, goals, and objectives; and finally provide consultation services that the institutions could not individually or collectively provide for themselves. He recommended to the state board that the role of the department would be limited to being an administrative agency of the board. Blake's plans to shake up the department, which included cutting back roughly 25 percent of the 205 employees in the department, met with rigorous pushback on the part of some. His plans to eliminate the area coordinators' program did away with the job of one board member and the job of the brother of another. But more importantly, it raised the ire of former chairman Dallas Herring, who in a speech at James Sprunt Community College in Kenansville, stated, "Dismissal of extension educators, while politically understandable, is not justified educationally except in the view of those who oppose total education." He went on to state that he feared that the college-level general education programs in the technical institutes might be lost. He warned, "I hope it is not because they reach the otherwise unreached, for this is a duty which the state owes to no man, if it does not owe it to all men." Fortunately for the system, Herring's warnings did not go unheeded. Both he and David Gillespie of the *News and Observer* continued to speak and write on behalf of "total education." As Gillespie wrote, "The dismal statistics relating educational attainment to income in North Carolina show that Blake and his board can fill an enormous need that exists in North Carolina, not just for job training, but education—period."

Meanwhile President Blake and the board continued to emphasize vocational and job training, some feared at the expense of the fledging college transfer function. The legislation establishing the State Board of Community Colleges had also put in place a more official tie between the office of the state president of the Department of Community Colleges and the office of the governor. Plus Governor Hunt, according to some, had played a role in Blake's selection as president and was seen as one of his supporters. So when the governor sent a letter to Blake on February 8, 1980, Blake quickly responded with a report titled "The North Carolina Community College System: Status and Trends." In that report Blake stated, "In full commitment to a priority of vocational-technical training, enrollments in community colleges and technical institutes over the past ten years have increased substantially in that area while declining in college transfer." Actually, though enrollments in vocational-technical training had increased dramatically (255 percent) from 1969 to 1979, college transfer had increased as well (60 percent). Committed state legislative support along with additional federal funding had made the difference.

The report also showed a system coming of age and even more focused on vocation-technical training. During the previous decade, an analysis of the training provided showed that vocational-technical training had increased from 65 percent to 73 percent, adult basic education had declined from 14 percent to 8 percent, and college transfer declined from 12 percent to 6 percent. All "other" programs had increased from 10 percent to 13 percent. The student population was changing as well. In the early days of the system, most students were male and predominantly white. As of 1979 female enrollment exceeded 53 percent, minority enrollment exceeded 23 percent, and part-time enrollment had increased to over 21 percent. The median age for curriculum students was twenty-five years, and 40 percent of them had some college.

In a speech to the Northwest North Carolina Development Association in the spring of 1980, Governor Hunt continued to stress the need for vocational-technical training in the system. He stated that he planned to ask the General Assembly for $1 million for "cooperative apprenticeship" programs involving industry at both the community colleges and schools. But even with the continued focus on job preparation, a budget increase of $683,808 was approved by the board to fund additional college transfer programs at fifteen local institutions, including College of the Albemarle, Southeastern Community College, and Sandhills Community College. The board, in a resolution, also requested the legislature to correct its oversight in failing to fund Brunswick Technical Institute for 1980–81. And it approved Dr. Phail Wynn, a U.S. Army veteran, as the interim president of Durham Technical Institute, effective May 1, 1980. He would be the first African American appointed as a community college president later that year, and he would serve in that role until he retired in 2007.

The Department of Community Colleges was already studying and highlighting the challenges facing the growing number of community college transfer students. In a report titled "Guidelines for Transfer: Recommendations of the Joint Committee on College Transfer Student," dated April 1980, the director of college transfer and general education for the Department of Community Colleges, Bobby L. Anderson, along with four others on the editorial subcommittee pointed out that the 10,601 undergraduate transfer students who enrolled in North Carolina's colleges and universities in the fall of 1978 made up 10.3 percent of the total undergraduate population of the state. However, these students faced significant challenges in that there was a serious lack of consensus among colleges in North Carolina regarding general education and transfer procedures. By 1980 there were seventy-seven colleges and universities, thirty-five technical institutes, and more than sixty other postsecondary schools of business, trade, health, and religion. The circumstance, according to the authors, justified "a serious effort to bring some degree of standardization" into the transfer process. Many more years would pass before this would occur, but community colleges would remain at the forefront of those calling for change.

On September 5, 1980, in the House chamber of the capitol, the new State Board of Community Colleges (SBCC) was formally established. The charter board members, recognized by Governor Jim Hunt and sworn in by Chief Justice Joseph Branch, were Carl Horn Jr. (chairman), Stacy Budd (vice chairman), Richard L. Daugherty, Alan E. Thomas, Sam L. Wiggins, Charles E. Branford, Ronald E. Deal, James H. Martin Jr., Melvin C. Swann Jr., Martha N. Granger, Edward J. High, H. Clifton Blue, Isobel Craven Lewis, William J. Debrule, N. Elton Aydlett, I. J. Williams, and Lynn N. Kelso (in absentia). Lieutenant Governor James C. Green Jr. and state treasurer Harlan E. Boyles would serve as ex officio board members. Helen B. Dowdy was introduced by Dr. Larry Blake as the board's new secretary. After being briefed by President Blake on the community college system, the SBCC accepted an invitation from the State Board of Education (SBE) to meet jointly until year's end.

At the final meeting that year, on December 4, SBE chairman H. David Bruton turned over the gavel to SBCC chairman Carl Horn as a symbolic transfer of governance that occurred later, on January 1, 1981. At that meeting, President Larry Blake read a proclamation by Governor Hunt in which the governor stated,

> Whereas the community college system is entering into an exciting new era, with a new governing board, a new president, and a sense of mission; whereas the system is being called upon to rise to even greater challenges, principally to fulfill the role as the State's major resource in training North Carolina's people for the thousands of

high-skill, high-wage jobs that will bring about a new industrial revolution; therefore I proclaim 1981 as "The Year of the Community College in North Carolina."

At its first meeting in January 1981, the new board appointed its first presidents, Dr. Ben F. Currin as president of Vance-Granville Community College and Dr. Edward H. Wilson Jr. as president of Roanoke-Chowan Technical Institute. It also reappointed Dr. Larry J. Blake as state president of the Department of Community Colleges, effective January 1.

Ten days after those appointments, Governor Jim Hunt gave his second inaugural speech in Raleigh, wherein he outlined a new priority for the community college system. He stated, "We have significantly reduced the number of dropouts from our schools over the past few years. Now we must redouble our efforts and stress joint programs between our public schools and community colleges. The state of Charles Brantley Aycock and Terry Sanford should not rest until we help every single North Carolina youngster to graduate." It would be a challenge he would repeat on more than one occasion. And in many ways, it was prophetic of the Early College High Schools that would spring up on many community college campuses in North Carolina over twenty years later.

In February, Dr. Ronald W. Shearon of N.C. State University's Department of Adult and Community College Education presented a summary of his research on North Carolina's community college students to the new State Board of Community Colleges. Shearon found that the system was now serving an older population than it did a decade before. The median age for curriculum students was twenty-five, whereas those in continuing education averaged thirty-eight years of age. Over half of the students in curriculum programs were female (54 percent) and almost three-quarters of those in continuing education programs (71 percent) were female. As for race, Shearon found that enrollments in curriculum and continuing education programs matched the racial distribution found in the North Carolina adult population.

Other interesting findings by Shearon were that community college students were coming into the system with more education. His research showed that over the previous decade, fewer students were enrolling without a high school diploma; in fact, nearly 12 percent of all students in the system held a baccalaureate degree. However, his research showed that system primarily was serving a working student interested in learning. Over one-half of the curriculum and continuing education students worked either full- or part-time. Over 72 percent of the curriculum students were enrolled in technical or vocational programs, and over 50 percent of the continuing education students were taking occupational extension courses.

Technical or vocational training programs often required expensive equipment, which presented a challenge for community colleges seeking to offer such training. State treasurer Harlan Boyles had pointed out to the board, in a request titled "Community Colleges: A Proposal for Equipment Acquisition," that the department had made a request for $35 million to acquire new and replacement equipment. He suggested that the board set up an equipment acquisition fund and distribution system. And in April, the board attempted to respond to this need by endorsing a bill that would authorize the board to issue revenue bonds to purchase equipment for the system. Vice Chairman Stacy Budd was directed to arrange for the introduction of the bill in the General Assembly at the appropriate time.

Governor Hunt certainly supported this initiative as he sought to bring new industry and jobs to the state. In a speech to the Community College Congress in Raleigh in May he stated, "We have to equip our citizens with the skills they need to get and hold good jobs. That is, I believe, the primary issue before this congress and before this community college system." He went on to suggest that the state should set "our sights on making North Carolina a center for high technology industry." He stated that the community colleges should be the presumptive deliverers of skill training in North Carolina and that he was committed to pressing for the state resources that would enable the system to fulfill that responsibility. To do so would require a significant investment in the necessary equipment required to conduct the training, as well as qualified instructors. As such, he reminded business leaders at the Profit Through Innovation Conference in September that community colleges suffered from serious shortages of equipment, with some classes using equipment that dated back to World War II. He pointed out that many electronics classes were using early solid-state equipment, which was "like the stone age compared to today's state of the art." However, the governor pointed out that some industries had stepped forward to and loaned or donated equipment to their local community colleges to remedy the problems. He also suggested that businesses consider an executive or technician loan program to the faculty of local community colleges to help the colleges keep good instructors. President Blake, he promised, would "be as flexible as possible" in working out any arrangement. The governor stated, "With better equipment and more good instructors, we can take a quantum leap in the number of students truly qualified to work for your companies and others."

That same month, September 18, 1981, the board began a fall retreat at the Blockade Runner Motor Hotel in Wrightsville Beach. The board adopted guidelines to govern North Carolina's training program for new and expanding industry, which included policy on how the department was to allot funds to institutions. In its guidance, the board mandated that the state-funded training service would train incoming production employees of a new or expanding manufacturing industry with job skills so that new industries would be encouraged to locate in North Carolina or existing industries would be encouraged to expand. The people of North Carolina would be offered "specific training necessary to qualify for these new production jobs," and each new and expanding industry would be helped to create "a productive work force as expeditiously and as efficiently as possible." The guidelines for the new service stated that it would be made available to any new or expanding industry which promised to create a minimum of twelve new production jobs in North Carolina.

Even as the department sought to support the governor's vision of creating new jobs and supporting new and expanding industry, it did so with limited funding, particularly in comparison to other states and even to the other educational systems within the state. State treasurer Harlan Boyles pointed out, "The institutions of higher education [university system] have been more successful with their activities in the General Assembly." In 1980–81, the public schools received 44.2 percent ($1.4 billion), the UNC system got 16.5 percent ($515.2 million), and only 5.6 percent ($175.7 million) went to the community college system. Even with constraints on funding, the colleges produced training meeting the needs of North Carolinians. A survey of community college students from the prior year (1979–80) showed that 78.6 percent of respondents felt that their occupational courses were "good" or "very good," and 70 percent of those who graduated felt that their training was "related to their present occupation."

In a move that was reminiscent of the opposition of private colleges to the community colleges in the late 1950s, private colleges along with the Council for Higher Education of the Western North Carolina Conference of the United Methodist Church, successfully opposed the addition of a college transfer program at Guilford Technical Institute in Jamestown in March 1982. Surprisingly enough, one of the opponents was former governor Dan Moore, who wrote to Guilford commissioner Paul Clapp, "The original idea of the technical institutes across the state was, as their name implies, to give technical training to those who are not interested in going to a liberal arts college. As a former governor I have been concerned with the trend to make these institutions colleges." Moore went on to say that he felt such should not be done unless there was a definite need for additional opportunities for colleges or universities. The executive secretary of the North Carolina Center for Independent Higher Education, Ralph Byers, shared Moore's concern and stated, "If that request is approved, there will be absolutely no grounds for disallowing any other technical institute from becoming a community college, and we'll have fifty-eight community colleges." Later both fears would be realized.

Also during this period, the State Board of Community Colleges began to be concerned with the transferability of community college credits. Chairman Carl Horn announced in April that he planned to discuss the problem of transferability of credit with representatives of the state's private colleges and universities as well as President William C. Friday, the leader of the University of North Carolina. The discussion grew out of the Guilford Tech controversy and the board's realization that lack of transferability was seriously hindering the educational advancement of community college graduates. At least two decades would pass, however, before the board and its allies would be able to deal effectively with the issue. In fact, later that summer Dr. Marc D. Allred, the department's vice president for planning and research services, bemoaned the fact that the community colleges were unable to increase the number of African American students transferring to traditionally white universities. This element of the revised desegregation plan, which was a part of an agreement between the University of North Carolina and the U.S. Department of Education, was approved by the board in August. Allred suggested that the reason the goal had not been met was not due to departmental intransigence, but because there was a trend generally away from college transfer and toward vocational and technical training. While African American enrollment was up around 3 percent in the previous year, the total of students of all races had decreased by 396.

State president Larry Blake continued to focus the energies and funds of the community college toward vocational education. In the fall of 1982 Blake announced that the three explicit goals of the North Carolina Community College System were to provide training in the skills demanded by the modern economy, provide comprehensive learning opportunities for all people of North Carolina, and eliminate illiteracy and raise the level of educational attainment. But even as the colleges attempted to respond to job training and educational needs, they faced budget cuts in the fall of that year. A total of $12 million in funding to the system was trimmed, with the range of reductions spanning from Central Piedmont Community College in Charlotte facing a reduction of $1.04 million to Pamlico Technical College losing $45,000.

As the year came to a close, the community college system again faced a major change in leadership that portended a future change in direction. At the December 9 board meeting, the State Board of Community Colleges went into executive session to discuss a personnel matter with President Blake—namely his consideration of other jobs. Blake had already announced publicly that he was a finalist for presidency of the Oregon Institute of Technology at Klamath Falls and Western Oregon State College. In less than two weeks, he announced that he was leaving North Carolina for Klamath Falls. He stated, "As we move into the future based on high technology, the institutions of technology will play a more important role." Interestingly enough, the presidency at Oregon Institute of Technology came with more than an eight-thousand-dollar pay cut. He was to assume the position in March 1983.

Almost immediately, speculation began as to who would replace Blake. Some of the names mentioned included Dr. Jeff Hockaday, president of Central Carolina Technical College in Sanford; Dr. Raymond A. Stone, president of Sandhills Community College; and Dr. John L. Tart, a member of the State Board of Education and the president of Johnston Technical College in Smithfield. Also mentioned as a possible replacement was former governor Bob Scott, who was still interested in the job.

One of President Blake's last actions prior to leaving North Carolina was to urge the board at its February meeting to oppose the state House of Representatives bill, which would give to the legislature the final say on hiring the system's presidents. Blake wanted that authority to be returned to the State Board of Community Colleges. The legislature in 1981 had given the governor final approval authority. Hunt announced through his press secretary, Gary Pearce, that he planned to remain strictly neutral, particularly as Scott had emerged as a front runner to replace Blake. At that same February board meeting, Blake pointed out that during his three-and-one-half-year tenure, he had overseen, among other accomplishments, closer linkages between the system and business and industry, successful transition from the State Board of Education to the new State Board of Community Colleges, a change in program emphasis to flexible funding for critical needs, and establishment of a more flexible cooperative skills on-the-job training program for business and industry. However, an enrollment report at the meeting indicated that the total unduplicated headcount enrollment of the system the previous year was 601,124, a reduction of approximately 1 percent from the year prior.

On March 1, 1983, the State Board of Community Colleges held a special meeting to elect a new system president. Board chair Carl Horn announced, "We'd like to have somebody who commands respect in the General Assembly." He went on to say that the system needed $30 million to replace worn-out equipment and they did not want to have to use the $20 million in the budget for that purpose. Search Committee chair Lynn N. Kelso reminded the board that they should select whichever one of the finalists could "best carry forward the policies of this governing board" with fifty-eight presidents and fifty-eight boards of trustees internally and then externally with the legislature, administration, and all the citizens of North Carolina. The board interviewed both finalists in executive session: Dr. Johnas F. "Jeff" Hockaday and former governor Robert Scott. Afterward, upon the motion of Search Committee chair Kelso, with a second by Edward J. High, the board unanimously elected Robert W. "Bob" Scott as president. John Tart was selected to serve as interim president until Scott assumed his duties on March 7.

Scott and others greeted his selection with delight. Dr. John T. Caldwell, chancellor emeritus of N.C. State, remarked, "He's the right man in the right place at the right time." And Scott himself simply said, "I feel so good I don't know what to say." However, he would later state, "I'm pleased with the confidence that's been placed in me, and I'm pleased that I can share in this system's future growth." When some questioned the choice of a skilled politician over a professional educator, Chair Carl Horn pointed out that neither Bill Friday nor Terry Sanford were professional educators, but they were recognized leaders in their fields and few questioned their success. Horn went on to cite Scott's "high standing throughout the state," as well as his knowledge of the state budget and the interrelationships of the public schools, community college, and university systems. The fact remained that his strong political reputation and his ability to work with the General Assembly were just the traits the board had wisely foreseen would be required in the years ahead.

Even as the system looked ahead, it paused to look back. On May 17, at the Marriott Hotel in Raleigh, seven individuals who had significantly contributed to the establishment and growth of the community college system were honored at a twentieth-anniversary banquet. These were the original recipients of an honor that would eventually come to be called the I.E. Ready Award. They were Herbert Clifton Blue, Wallace William Gee, William Dallas Herring, James Eubert Holshouser Jr., William Donald "Billy" Mills, Issac Epps Ready, and Terry Sanford.

Even as the system looked back, further changes lay ahead in leadership and direction. In May, SBCC chairman Carl Horne Jr. had announced his retirement, effective June 30, in that he would not be accepting reappointment by Governor Hunt to a second term. According to Horn, he felt the time was the right for his departure as he was optimistic about the system's future, that it was in good hands with former governor Scott at the helm, and that it even appeared that the crisis in funding for new equipment was soon to be resolved. The board passed a resolution in his honor that concluded by stating, "Be it resolved therefore that the North Carolina Community College System, in gratitude that cannot equal Carl's value to us, expresses its sincerest appreciation for what he means to us personally and to the thousands of North Carolina citizens who have benefited from his labors." The next morning, June 10, 1983, Governor Jim Hunt hosted a breakfast in his honor at the Radisson Plaza Hotel in Raleigh.

John A. Forelines Jr., chairman and president of the Bank of Granite and one of two new Hunt appointees to the State Board of Community Colleges, was sworn in at the July meeting of the board. Other new appointees included Barbara K. Allen, Robert Z. Hawkins, William S. Murdoch, and William C. Parton. Vice Chairman Lynn Kelso announced during elections that it was the governor's intention that Forelines become chairman, after which he was nominated and elected. The board, in a move to address needed continuity and efficiency in administration of the system, approved the establishment of an executive vice president. Dr. Edward H. Wilson Jr., the president of Roanoke-Chowan Technical Institute, was named by President Scott to fill that role. Wilson's father had been a former legislator and an early supporter of Dallas Herring's vision of a strong and comprehensive community college system. Ed Wilson Sr. had been active in the department during the Fountain presidency, and as such, Dr. Wilson was no stranger to North Carolina's community colleges. He proved to be a tireless worker and advocate for the growing system.

Both Governor Hunt and system president Scott continued to stress the need for high-technology training, to be provided primarily by the community colleges. At the beginning of the year, in his State of the State Address, Hunt had reminded the General Assembly that they needed to provide the necessary funding so that the system could purchase the equipment needed for training. He stated, "The primary responsibility of our community college system must be to teach people the skills they need to get good jobs, and we must see that this responsibility is being met." As Hunt pointed out in his address to the Community College Conference on High Technology at Raleigh on November 21, 1983, the legislature had responded to his challenge by allocating $28 million in new equipment, $19.6 million for new enrollment, and $12.6 million for new industries. New partnerships between industry and community colleges had sprung up across the state. They included Asplundh and Vance-Granville Community College, Bendix and Gaston College, Central Piedmont and Verbatim, and Durham Tech together with Mitsubishi and Sumitomo. Furthermore, new programs being established throughout the system included a new robotics curriculum at Catawba Valley Technical College and new industrial management and maintenance programs that Forsyth Tech would be offering to twenty-year employees at Western Electric. Hunt concluded, "As the foundation of North Carolina's economy, you are the key to its future."

President Scott agreed. However, he was concerned that high school students were coming into the system unprepared for the challenge of the high-technology curricula. In an address at Blue Ridge Technical College earlier that year, Scott bemoaned the fact that "you cannot teach anyone high technology unless he can read, write, and compute to begin with." He was also concerned that in an attempt to respond to the need for high-tech training in the tight economy and dislocation of workers created by the Sun Belt high-tech boom, legislators were beginning to ask for special legislation targeted to specified community colleges. This development would prove to be one of the great challenges that the system and its new president would face.

Declining enrollments and desegregation were two other challenges Scott and the system faced as well. In 1983 the legislature had increased tuition and fees at community colleges. One result, at least system leaders maintained, was a reduction in enrollment. Tentative fall-quarter enrollments indicated that FTE numbers were down 8.9 percent and unduplicated headcount was down 3.3 percent. As a result, actual collection of tuition and fees was 12.7 percent lower than the amount budgeted for the first half of the fiscal year.

Meanwhile, a letter from Harry Singleton, an assistant secretary for civil rights at the U.S. Department of Education, had expressed continued concern with inadequate enrollment of black students in the college transfer program and employment of black academic personnel. The department was also concerned that more African Americans were not appointed to institutional governing boards. The NCCCS office responded in part that "the college transfer program was not conceived as the major purpose of the community college system." In addition, when one evaluated total system enrollments, which included the technical institutes, the college transfer enrollment had dropped from 12 percent in 1969–70 to 7.2 percent. Even given this challenging scenario, the department pledged to develop a "desegregation plan" to address federal concerns. That plan, approved in February 1984, included the completion of a retention study, the development of a student recruitment manual focused on minorities, and other activities designed to increase African American professional employment and student enrollment in the college transfer program.

Throughout the early years of his administration, Scott and his team would attempt to bring unity and focus to the administration and funding of the community college system. In November 1983 Chairman John Forlines spoke to a joint meeting of the North Carolina Industrial Developers Association and the Association of Public Community College Presidents in Raleigh. He warned that special bills in the General Assembly giving some local colleges extra funding jeopardized the unity of the system. He stated, "New programs and new facilities that are the result of political jockeying rather than sound educational and economic planning are not in the best interests of our state or community college system."

President Scott's political prowess paid early and continuing dividends for the community colleges in dealing with these and other challenges. In the spring of 1984 Scott reported to the board that the U.S. Department of Education had accepted the Desegregation Plan for the system. Furthermore, budgetary successes in dealings with the legislature had resulted in $28 million over the biennium for equipment, nearly $20 million for enrollment growth, and a doubling of funds allocated for new and expanding industry. But he remained concerned over present and planned tuition increases, noting that the continued proliferation of special funding bills was damaging system unity.

Unity, along with economic development, was the focus of the new governor, James Grubbs Martin, who was inaugurated in Raleigh on January 5, 1985. Martin, only the second Republican to hold that office in the twentieth century, called for a new birth of unity in economic development, education, and political freedom. He concluded, "With its problems, its opportunities, and its challenges, the future calls us together." Fortunately, during his first term (1985–89), North Carolina would enjoy a period of unprecedented economic growth. More than 380,000 jobs were created, and new and expanding investment totaled more than $21 billion. Community colleges would be both the beneficiaries and supporters of that growth.

In 1984-85, the number of small business centers (SBCs) had risen to fourteen and were strategically located across the state. The program, which began during the Hunt years, was established to provide accessible and comprehensive educational and informational services to small business owners through a statewide network. The centers positioned community colleges as clearinghouses of information for small business owners, including the development of continuing education courses, linkage networks, and curriculum programs. In 1984 funding was provided for centers at Carteret Technical College, Central Piedmont Community College, College of the Albemarle, Davidson County Community College, Gaston College, Guilford Technical Community College, Lenoir Community College, and Roanoke Chowan Technical College. The following year would see the addition of six more SBCs. This program would be highlighted in issue papers prepared for the new governor, Jim Martin.

Governor Martin would soon be adding his voice to that of President Scott and Chairman Forlines in calling for unity of purpose in funding the community colleges. On February 19, 1985, Scott told both the Senate and House Higher Education Committees that politically strong colleges were gaining funding at the expense of those that were politically weak, creating inequities in the system. He decried the resulting atmosphere of tension and mistrust created among system administrators. He declared, "In such an atmosphere, long-range planning becomes an exercise in futility." In April, Chairman Forlines would warn the State Board of Community Colleges that he believed the practice of funding some at the expense of others would "ultimately do great damage to the community college system." The next month, at a speech to the North Carolina Association of Community College Trustees, Governor Jim Martin expressed his concern about the special bills by saying, "We have seen some institutions achieve remarkable gains at the expense of the system as a whole. The political haves benefit at the expense of the political have-nots." The governor felt it was time to put an end to such practices.

During Governor Martin's two terms (1985–93), the community college system under Scott's able leadership pressed ahead on multiple fronts. In addition to successfully dealing with the issue of special bills, the system continued to grapple with other difficult issues such as the right of its graduates to be accepted as transfer students by universities and colleges within the state. In fact, during discussion in April with UNC officials about the community college system taking over remedial training, President Scott suggested that the system would be willing to entertain the idea if the university system would, in turn, accept community college transfer students. The following month, Scott met with military base commanders and military education service officers of the four major military operations at Coastal Carolina Community College. They discussed how the community colleges might better serve the needs of the military. Problems unique to that population included the need for greater flexibility in scheduling and, again, the transfer of credit.

Under Scott's leadership during the governor's first term, the system had secured additional funding, including a 10 percent salary increase for state employees and $26 million for construction. He had worked with institutions to successfully meet the requirements of the Desegregation Plan, his top priority; to develop initiatives to support existing industry and law enforcement training; and to promote adult literacy. In fact, over 49,000 students were served during 1984–85 alone, an increase of 27 percent over the previous year. Undoubtedly, part of the reason for the increase was Scott's commitment to partner with religious leaders to increase public awareness and enrollment in adult literacy programs. In fact, at a meeting in Raleigh the previous year, over one hundred ministers had signed a scroll pledging to help identify and enroll illiterate church members. Scott's genuine plea that as educators "we're not always able to convey to these people that we do want to help" had resulted in people of faith stepping forward to help.

Success came in other areas as well, particularly in the allied health fields. In October 1985 Scott reported to the State Board of Community Colleges that students from thirty-one local institutions had taken nursing board examinations to be licensed as a registered nurse. Of those students, 859 had passed the boards, resulting in a 91 percent passing rate. Furthermore, six institutions—Caldwell Community College and Technical Institute, College of the Albemarle, Gaston College, Rockingham, Western Piedmont, and Wilkes Community College—had 100 percent of their candidates pass the exam.

In support of business training and partnerships with industry, the system continued to expand its role. When a delegation of Japanese business leaders visited in April 1986, Governor Martin was able to point to the North Carolina Community College System as one of the reasons Japanese businesses should consider investing in North Carolina. He told the Keidanren (Japanese Federation of Economic Organizations) delegation that the community colleges were "rated among our country's leading centers of training and retraining for the modern world of work. Twenty of them have established small business centers to provide intensive assistance to entrepreneurial enterprises."

The North Carolina Community College Foundation was also born in the spring of 1986. At its March meeting, the State Board of Community Colleges authorized a charter, by-laws, and guidelines for the new foundation. Established to secure funds from private donors to support a variety of developmental activities, the board made it clear that it was not to compete with the foundations that existed at fifty-six of the fifty-eight community colleges. Later, D. M. Lauch Faircloth of Clinton would be named president of the foundation and Patricia H. Holshouser of Southern Pines, the wife of former governor Holshouser, was named vice president.

Also during that year, five regional workshops were held throughout North Carolina for the purpose of improving and clarifying the process of transfers of students between the UNC and the NCCC systems. Counselors and admissions officers from both systems attended the workshops. In addition, participants received a thorough review of the university's new admission requirements.

The following year, 1987, saw the system continue to grow even as it rededicated itself to its past heritage. At a joint meeting on January 8 with the State Board of Education, President Scott reminded the SBCC and SBE members that it was former SBE chairman Dr. W. Dallas Herring who laid out the philosophy that guided the system throughout its early years. Scott went on to cite the goals set forth in the 1976 Commission on the Future report, which stated that the system remained dedicated to comprehensive adult education, focused primarily on vocational, technical, and basic education for adults. Less than two weeks later, Governor Martin would announce to the North Carolina Job Training Coordinating Council meeting in Raleigh that he felt that training must start even earlier. Pointing out that there existed a compelling need to upgrade our technical skills training programs, the governor stated that he supported the "two-plus-two" program in which a high school student spends two years acquiring the applied basic foundation necessary to support two years of instruction at the community college in highly technical skills. Now referred to as Tech Prep, Martin supported the newly designed program and stated, "I am told that the Department of Community Colleges and the Department of Public Instruction, the latter through its Vocational Education Program, are moving in this direction, and I am delighted that progress is being made."

The last two years of the governor's first term saw further innovations and enhancements. The Department of Community Colleges would seek and receive membership in the Southern Association of Colleges and Schools (SACS), and a new collaborative pharmaceutical technology program linking Nash Technical College, Wilson Technical College, and Wake Technical College was established. The program was developed in cooperation with several pharmaceutical companies, including Abbot Laboratories in Rocky Mount, Merck Sharp & Dohme in Wilson, and Glaxo Inc. in Zebulon. It came about due to the needs of these companies as well as thirty-seven industrial firms in the surrounding area, referred to at that time as Triangle East.

An isolated case of fraud at Cape Fear Technical College had led to a State Bureau of Investigation probe of several colleges in the system. As a result, the system took a much closer look at financial procedures, and President Scott warned the system that he believed that they had been too timid in dealing with the problem. He stated, "I firmly believe that our institutions should be allowed as much autonomy and flexibility as possible, consistent with good management and accountability practices that will protect our credibility and will assure public confidence." The board authorized President Scott and his department to develop and bring corrective proposals for legislative consideration to the board.

Later that year, the board authorized a Commission on the Future as a result of the audit findings and legislative action allowing colleges to adopt new names. Basically, Representative William T. Watkins of Granville sponsored a measure that would allow the remaining thirty-two technical institutes to become community colleges offering college transfer courses. The bill, which received the backing of a majority of the House, and later the Senate, limited transfer courses to no more than 15 percent of a college's offerings. Surprisingly enough, John T. Henley, president of the North Carolina Association of Independent Colleges and Universities, did not view it as much of a threat and did not oppose it. President Scott endorsed the bill, which passed the legislature on July 2. Watkins's hope was that the technical colleges might gain some prestige out of the new titles, and community college leaders saw a broader opportunity for college transfer students. Regardless, board leadership realized it was time again to evaluate where the system was and where it was headed. As President Scott stated, "What's happening is...our system has undergone a period of rapid growth, and it took everything we had to just stay on top of that growth. Now that growth is largely behind us and the rate has leveled off. With that comes stability." In fact, Scott saw the Commission on the Future of the North Carolina Community College System as a way of facing the serious questions of the future role of the state's newest higher education system. Scott stated that he hoped the commission would serve to revitalize the system. He was fearful that the system would become too traditional or complacent. He did not want the community colleges joining the Ivy League in outlook or purpose. He stated, "I don't guess we'll ever have ivy growing around our towers, but we can get some kudzu."

The end of the decade would see the colleges in the system embrace college transfer and change their names to include the term "community college." Likewise, the twenty-three member Commission on the Future announced at a news conference on November 20, 1988, that it would meet over the course of the next eighteen months. Led by Carolina Power and Light chairman Sherwood H. Smith Jr., the panel was charged by President Scott with taking a "hard look" at the community college system. According to Scott, no area was to be considered off limits as they studied the system. At the commission's first meeting Scott listed five paradoxes or philosophical contradictions that needed study: job skills training but general education, high quality but affordable access, local flexibility but state control, unique local needs but equitably distributed resources, and commendable service but serious underfunding. These areas would guide the group in the months that followed.

The community college system continued to focus its primary efforts on technical and vocational training. In 1988–89, the board funded and began, at Governor Jim Martin's request, Focused Industrial Training with an addition of $2 million to its expansion budget request. As he stated at a meeting of the High Point Chamber of Commerce on December 5, 1989, his intention was to provide the training to encourage development. He said, "A number of companies here have also taken advantage of the technical training program offered by Guilford Technical Community College. When you expand or retool, we pledge to train your employees, your way, at our expense. Now that's what I call a good deal."

Many felt that this should remain and possibly become the sole focus of the system. "The Bridge to the Next Century," a twenty-four-page report for the Commission on the Future by a panel of educators, economists, and business leaders from outside of the state, concluded that community colleges would soon be called upon to retrain workers for high-tech jobs. It recommended that the system stop trying to be all things to all people and concentrate on providing adults with the basic academic, technical, and vocational skills they needed to be ready for the jobs of the future. Their viewpoint was shared, to a lesser degree, by William C. Friday, president emeritus of the UNC System and president of the William R. Kenan Jr. Fund. He told the commission in late August 1988 that the community colleges should work to develop the state's supply of human capital and that, to do so adequately, the system's mission should be refined. Friday warned, "You can't be all things to all people. That day is over."

As Scott had promised, every area was on the table, which made many uncomfortable. In addition to Dr. Friday, the commission heard from the presidents and trustees of colleges. They were wary of any change in governance that might centralize control of the system. The chairman of the board of trustees at Central Piedmont warned that such a move "will serve to destroy the strength of the North Carolina Community College System." However, many trustees and presidents welcomed discussion of a change to the FTE formula, which they felt led to an FTE chase that subverted academic priorities. Such talk caused Dr. Dallas Herring, the acknowledged father of the system, to weigh in and warn against tampering with the formula. He worried that methodology that awarded funds based upon the cost of programs would result in more prestigious, expensive programs being generated, "with the result that thousands with less expensive needs will be neglected." He went on to remind the leaders, "These institutions are not graduate schools for the elite. They are the workingman's university."

With much fanfare, the Commission on the Future released its report in February 1989. The panel proposed changes that would result in increased management flexibility and resources. The report also pointed to a need for increased accountability, stating, "We have the system in place to meet many of the needs of our state. What we are proposing is that the System be modified and strengthened to better meet the challenges of the future." To accomplish this, the commission report, titled "Gaining the Competitive Edge," contained recommendations including

- An increase in funding tied to stronger accountabilities for the results achieved.
- A renewed emphasis on teaching basic English, mathematics, and conceptual thinking skills that will be demanded by the workplace of the future.
- A reaffirmation of the commitment to build state and local economies through spreading new technology into the workplace and by supporting the development of small business.
- Clarification of the relationship between the individual colleges and the state board and the Department of Community Colleges staff to provide for flexibility for local institutions while requiring accountability for the system as a whole.
- Development of strong partnerships with public schools and other institutions of higher learning to establish a comprehensive education system that is responsive to all of North Carolina's needs.

Governor Martin referred to the report as excellent and suggested that it would be the blueprint for the future to determine "where we need to be going with this brilliant resource of our fifty-eight community colleges."

C. Neill McLeod, President, Martin Community College, 1979–1982 (First female NC community college president)

Phail Wynne Jr., President— Durham Technical Community College, 1980-2007 (First African-American NC community college president)

Edgar J. Boone, William Dallas Herring Distinguished Professor Emeritus and department chair of Adult and Community College Education—1963–1991, NC State University

Larry J. Blake, NCCCS President, 1979-1982

Robert W. Scott, NCCCS President, 1983-1995

*Choral group practicing at Rockingham
Community College, 1978*

*North Carolina State Board of Education meeting, fall 1973;
Lieutenant Governor Jim Hunt, center, foreground; President Ben Fountain,
2nd from left; Chairman Dallas Herring, 5th from left*

VII

Challenges and Changes

I have never changed what I thought years ago, that given the direct linkage between what you do in the community college, what you choose to do, and what the workplace out there needs, it [the community college system] is more important to the workplace than the universities are.

LLOYD "VIC" HACKLEY

Educational opportunity programs are all about opening doors. All of us have that commitment to opening doors in common.... More broadly it means that we understand the continuing and growing importance of access as one of the vital challenges of higher education.

MARTIN LANCASTER

Students aren't going to get where they need to be without the open door. But it can't be a revolving door. So that's why you see not just this enormous emphasis just on access, but success.

SCOTT RALLS

In 1993 Raleigh welcomed back to the governor's mansion a man who was no stranger to either it or community colleges. Jim Hunt, who had served as chairman of the State Board of Education with Dallas Herring during the formative years of the community college, had insisted that it remain true to its original mission of jobs and economic development. But in his inaugural address given on January 9, 1993, he reminded all North Carolinians, "Change will not be measured by what happens in Raleigh. It will be measured by what happens in your homes and in your communities. Change will not be measured by the laws we pass. It will be measured by the lives we touch"—eloquent words that could easily, particularly in its mention of communities, be applied to the role and work of North Carolina's community college system. Hunt would occupy the mansion and indeed be at the forefront of politics in North Carolina well into the next millennium. And he would place his stamp on education in North Carolina for the foreseeable future.

During that decade, which would see major changes in leadership and smaller ones in direction, Hunt and the system would continue to stress economic development. On February 11, 1993, during a speech to the Emerging Issues Forum in Raleigh, the governor would recount how in a trip to Greensboro for a ribbon cutting at a semiconductor computer chip manufacturer, he met a young employee during the plant tour who had developed a new microelectronic device. This device was responsible for the first American contract with NTT—Nippon Telegraph and Telephone Public Corp.—Japan's telephone company. As such, this young man was responsible for hundreds of jobs. Hunt recounted how when he asked him where he went to school, he expected him to respond with one of North Carolina's engineering schools, such as Hunt's alma mater, N.C. State. The young inventor proudly replied that he was a graduate of the Guilford County School System and that he had an associate degree from Guilford Technical Community College.

Hunt went on to argue that North Carolina had to invest not just in infrastructure and technology but, equally importantly, in its people. Hunt announced that in the next few days, by executive order, he would create the Governor's Commission on Workforce Preparedness. Furthermore, he would be asking the General Assembly to provide funding so that the Tech Prep program could be expanded into all one hundred counties. In addition, Hunt insisted that the state "upgrade our community college system's ability to provide the kind of education, training, and retraining that the workplace demands." He said that in recent years, North Carolina had fallen behind in adequately funding the system. He pointed out, "Today, community colleges get less than eight cents of the state's education dollar. Many campuses are turning away students for lack of space or teachers. Salaries are forty-seventh in the nation. Equipment has not kept pace with technology." Hunt said that his budget would include money to address these inequities, while still requiring that colleges maximize available resources.

The system accomplished this by partnering with existing and new industry. In January at a press conference in Cleveland, the governor pointed to just such a partnership. The Freightliner Corporation was expanding its operations in North Carolina, to include eight hundred more jobs. To do this successfully, the state was building a training center in Cleveland, at a cost of $3 million, to train not just Freightliner workers but thousands of workers from all over North Carolina. In addition, the state committed $3.6 million over the next three years to operate the center. This was one of the first Centers of Excellence to be established to train and retrain workers. Both the Government Performance Audit Committee (GPAC) and the Commission on the Future of Community Colleges had recommended regional training centers.

The center, dedicated on May 18, 1995, would have its schedule overseen by Freightliner, but it was available to many other workers. Rowan-Cabarrus and Gaston Community Colleges provided instructors and support for the center and utilized it for their students as well. The latest computer technology was provided to design and support courses. The impact of the new center was multiplied many times over by its connection to the new North Carolina Information Highway. It was, at that time, the most advanced telecommunications network in the world, capable of transmitting text, graphics, video, and voice communications. Five hundred million bits of data could be transmitted between locations, so complicated images could be transferred and interpreted instantly. Workers in distant areas would have what the governor referred to as "access to excellence." Such partnerships and pooling of resources would become more and more common in the community college system during the 1990s.

To support such expansion, North Carolinians had supported five statewide bond issues in November 1993. Thanks to strong backing from urban voters, all the measures but one—the economic development financing amendment—passed. The citizens supported $310 million for new classrooms, laboratories, and new facilities to support growing enrollment in the UNC system and $250 million for new classrooms in the community colleges. In addition they voted for $145 million for water-sewer projects and $35 million to improve state parks. Governor Hunt observed that the people of North Carolina had wisely chosen to invest in the state's future. "It will move our state forward when others are falling behind." The influx of money was critical to the success of the system well into the next century.

The following year, 1994, saw changes in leadership and a major first for the North Carolina Community College System. President Bob Scott, after serving for over a decade, announced his retirement at year's end, and the system began looking for his replacement. The three finalists announced that fall were retired IBM executive Richard Daugherty, Chancellor Geraldine Evans of the Minnesota Community College System, and Chancellor Lloyd "Vic" Hackley of Fayetteville State University. On October 14, 1994, the state board unanimously voted to name Dr. Hackley as the new president. In making the announcement board chair Lieutenant Governor Dennis Wicker stated, "When you look at all of what he had, all of his strengths, when you put those together, he stood above the rest." Hackley had been FSU's chancellor since 1988 and had formerly taught at the Government Executives Institute at the University of North Carolina at Chapel Hill and previous to that, at the University of Arkansas. He had also served as a vice president at UNC General Administration, where he counted Dr. Clemmie Dixon "Dick" Spangler, UNC System president, as a friend and strong supporter. Prior to coming to UNC, Hackley had a distinguished career in the U.S. Air Force that spanned two decades and included tours in Vietnam and as an instructor at the Air Force Academy.

Hackley was the first African American to head the North Carolina Community College System, but some, with Hackley among them, maintained that ethnicity had little to do with his election. Dr. Hackley stated, "If I had gotten a signal that this choice was being made because of... my parents, you'd be talking to somebody else. When it comes to being a first, I think I am the first person from Roanoke, Virginia, to head up a community college system." Hackley, who began his college career at a community college in Traverse City,

Michigan, went on to say that he looked forward to working with the board to take the North Carolina community college system to the next level. He predicted that community colleges "are going to change the education landscape more than any other element." He agreed that with the board that top priorities should be adult literacy and an educated workforce. However, he said that those tasks should not be narrowly focused, as workers in the future would need to be able to adapt to rapidly changing workplaces.

Hackley later stated that he wasn't that interested in the job at the beginning, but people whom he respected, including Bill Friday and Dick Spangler, told him that given what he had done at Fayetteville State, and the needs of the community college, he would be ideal for it and to allow his name to remain in contention. His supporters told him that they needed someone who could bring about a system that was more "tightly connected" with the university system. They envisioned, according to Hackley, a common course syllabi and a common course library,

> all those things that I believed in because when I went from Northwestern Michigan College [community college] down to Michigan State University, it was absolutely seamless. I went right into my junior year, no problem whatsoever—did better than the freshman and sophomores who had come to Michigan State as entering freshman, and I thought, *This is really smooth. This is the way it ought to work.* And so that's what I pushed when I went into the community college system office.
>
> Former president Scott had already begun moving the system in this direction, and Hackley and his team would continue the work.

Sharon Morrisey, who had begun working in the system office in 1992, had initiated those discussions while Bob Scott was president. She remembered,

> I started realizing that there were fifty-eight different college catalogs and that was part of the problem between and among community colleges.... And one day I went and met with Governor Scott and his senior team and ... proposed that we think about having a common course library for the North Carolina community college

system so that all fifty-eight colleges would use the same basic set of courses. And then I also proposed transitioning from a quarter calendar to a semester calendar.

Dr. Morrisey went on to say, "So President Scott took that idea and talked to the Presidents' Association about it. The next thing I knew we were moving forward with making these plans."

The next two years saw numerous person-hours and much money spent on the new articulation plan. Over fourteen hundred faculty members served on different writing teams, and a large staff at the central office was required to adequately oversee the project. According to Morrisey, Parker Chesson, chief of staff at the systems office, took an active role throughout the process and provided the necessary leadership to move the process forward. Morrisey met with Dr. Roy Carroll, vice president for planning and later senior vice president for academic affairs for the university system, and Myra Cain, associate vice president of academic affairs, both of whom proved to be strong supporters of the course transfer idea. Of course there were some, particularly among community college presidents, who were nervous about giving up the quarter calendar, because they felt that calendar was better for vocational and technical programs. Morrisey remembered,

> We worked through that because we were able to tell them that they're teaching the same stuff and if they wanted to, they could teach it in eight-week mini-semesters instead of the sixteen-week semester if they needed it to be shorter. So we pulled together faculty from many, many disciplines across the community college system and we developed our common course library. That was the first step and to rewrite the courses so they could be taught on a semester basis instead of a quarter basis.

This step had to be accomplished before they could even begin an in-depth conversation with the universities about a statewide articulation agreement.

Morrisey also remembers pushback from some university personnel as well. Some university personnel "didn't understand the quality and rigor that occurs in community college instruction. So there was a learning opportunity." She stated that they brought together university and community college faculty to look at what courses would transfer, and the result was a remarkable collegial learning experience on both sides. The comprehensive agreement was based on two premises; one was that all institutions would accept the academic integrity of other institutions. Since all community colleges were accredited by the Southern Association of Colleges and Schools (SACS) and all transfer courses required an instructor with at least a master's degree, their requirements mirrored the university's. The second foundational premise was the agreement on and development of a universal undergraduate general education core curriculum that all community colleges would teach, which could then be accepted as transfer credits by all sixteen universities. Consisting of forty-four semester hours, the universities agreed to accept this as the transfer core. And those two premises served as the secure foundation upon which the articulation agreement was constructed and accepted by all. The agreement was rolled out in 1997, and over the course of the ten-plus years that followed, over 102,000 students would successfully transfer to four-year institutions. It proved to be a great success and a major accomplishment of the short-lived Hackley administration.

President Hackley began encountering friction soon after becoming president of the North Carolina Community College System. As he recalled, "There was some resentment of my having assumed the presidency. There was fear, and I don't know if it was a big fear or small fear, but it was expressed that I was going to make the community college system subordinate to the university system, it would be a stepchild, an underling of that system." In response to the question of whether that ever entered his thinking, Hackley stated, "No, absolutely not. No, we've got different roles. And if we play them right, the whole state will be better off. But that died kind of hard." In addition, Hackley remembers that some were concerned that he never worked "in the community college and I didn't understand the community college mentality. I kept thinking, *Well, I attended one. That doesn't make me an expert, but I certainly know their value.*" He attempted to convince the naysayers that what he wanted to do was make the community colleges even more significant because they were "getting a short shrift."

In the end, some said that it was primarily the politics of the era and the office that led to Hackley's departure. The change to the semester system combined with Hackley's naturally forceful nature led some to fear, as stated above, that he was attempting to centralize control in Raleigh. And then the legislature became involved. He recalled speaking to three legislators at a meeting who told him "to go back to my office, don't touch any of the relationships between my office and the colleges, don't touch any of the staff, don't do anything about the staff in there...essentially to go over there sit on my hands and not do anything." On his way out of the door, Hackley maintains he told them, "Thank you very much for this dialog. I hope we'll continue to talk [he hadn't been in office very long] as important as this is to the community college system. But it would be irresponsible for me to leave this room with your thinking that I'm going to do exactly what you just told me to do. I'm going back to my office and do my job the way that I see it, because I'm the president." Hackley remembers that, not long after, that his boss, Lieutenant Governor Dennis Wicker called him in and expressed concern that Hackley had not shown enough deference to the legislators. They had accused him of arrogance. He stated that he was just honest with them. It was indicative of the turbulent months that lay ahead.

On January 9, 1997, after just two years at the helm, President Hackley announced that he would resign. He promised to stay on until June 30 or until a new president was found, whichever came first. C. D. Spangler, a supporter to the end, stated, "It was an almost undoable job, in that the organizational structure of the community college system limits the effectiveness of even a very strong president." Others, including Hackley, pointed to his association with the Clinton administration and the university system, and his background with a Historic Black College as negatives, in the minds of some, that he could not overcome. But he summed up his primary reason for leaving as follows:

> Though it is a very important role right there, it's kind of removed from education. It's more politics.... There were no students there, no faculty, no courses, and [you] sort of worked with the legislature to get the budget and do that kind of stuff. I didn't feel bad about leaving because I was finally convinced that the honorable core of the community college system wasn't there in Raleigh, it was

over there on Wake Tech's campus, it was out there in Carteret, out there in Greensboro. That's where education was taking place.

Hackley felt, "OK, we can find a good man, or a good woman, to run the [system] office in there, and I could go do something that I wanted to do."

The North Carolina Community College continued to grow even as the far-reaching changes Hackley and others had envisioned were implemented. Addressing the North Carolina Community College Futures Conference held in Raleigh on January 14, 1998, Governor Hunt declared that 1997 was " a tremendous year for the North Carolina Community College System." He pointed to the National Education Goals Panel's designation of North Carolina as the state that had done more to improve schools than any other. And the National Commission on Teaching and America's Future rated North Carolina as one of the top states in the nation in improving teaching in the classroom. Hunt stated, "We are indeed blessed to have the best system in the nation." He went on to stress that the excellence started at the top with outstanding leadership. By then, that leadership was found in the person of President Martin Lancaster.

―――

Harold Martin Lancaster was born in Wayne County, North Carolina, in 1943. He displayed an interest in politics at an early age, forming friendships with leading legislators such as Colonel Ned Delamar, one of the early architects and supporters of the community college system. Lancaster attended the University of North Carolina at Chapel Hill, entering the law school at UNC after his junior year as a Law Alumni Scholar. After graduating in 1967 he joined the navy as a judge advocate for a three-year tour, eighteen months of which were spent off the coast of Vietnam. He returned to his home state to practice law, leading to a distinguished political career in the North Carolina House of Representatives and in Congress, where he served on the Armed Services Committee. In the fall of 1995 President Bill Clinton nominated Martin Lancaster to be the assistant secretary of the army for civil works, an office he assumed the next year. However, fate had other plans for Martin Lancaster.

As Lancaster would later recall, "Alice and I were home one weekend [they maintained a home in North Carolina while he was assistant secretary in DC] and I got a call from Anne Turlington, who was then a member of the state board and a longtime friend and political supporter. And she asked, 'How would you like to be president of the community college system?' I told her that I had never thought about any such thing." Lancaster pointed out to her, however, while thinking out loud, how strongly he had supported the community colleges through the years, first as a legislator and then as a congressman—and the fact that Alice, his wife, had been a community college instructor throughout their entire married life had given him a special perspective about community colleges. In the end, he told Anne he would like to be considered but first he would need to discuss the move with his family. Lancaster remembered that they "took the girls [his two daughters attended high school just outside of DC] out to supper on Sunday night and talked about it. We didn't know whether they would like the idea.... They were enthusiastic about it and encouraged me to apply." He ended up submitting a letter of application with a resume attached to the State Board of Community Colleges, which had hired Robert Barringer to assist with the selection process.

After successfully completing a personality profile—the MMPI, which was required of all applicants—Lancaster was eventually named as one of three finalists. The other two finalists were long-serving, successful presidents of North Carolina community colleges: Don Cameron of Guilford Tech and Marvin Joyner of Central Carolina. Interviews were set up for early May 1998 with the full board. Lancaster remembered that the interview went very well, and one question—in view of the other finalists' qualifications—was no surprise. Board member Robert Green asked him, "Mr. Lancaster, what makes you think you can be president of the community college system when you've never worked a day in your life in the system?" Lancaster responded,

> Number one, though I have not worked in the system, I have been married to it throughout my life, and in addition to that, in my opinion, it's not really a question as to whether I have experience in the community college system. Really what is important for this job is leadership. Right now, I head the largest engineering firm in the world, and I'm not an engineer. It is really about vision, advocacy, leadership, working with people, being able to work with the

General Assembly and the Congress on behalf of the system. I can hire all the subject-matter experts that I need to fill in the blanks.

The secret to a successful presidency was never more succinctly put. Bob Jordan and the board certainly believed so, and Martin Lancaster was hired as the system's sixth leader. He reported to work on July 1, 1997.

During the rest of that year Lancaster set about creating his own leadership team at the system office. He kept on Scott Ralls, whom he remembered was working in Economic and Workforce Development. He would later make him a vice president of that area, and over a decade later, Scott would be his choice for president. He also retained Chancy Capp, though she was a Hackley hire from their days together at the university. He stated, "I knew how smart she was, and in fact she was one of the most important people on my team. She was director of external affairs and did a fantastic job." Martin stated that he decided to let go all of the other senior people from Hackley's staff, which proved to be a popular move with the presidents and the system office staff as well. Hackley had hired most of them from the university and had hired few "community college people." Lancaster set out to change that situation. He brought in Brenda Rogers from Durham Tech and Kennon Briggs from the state budget office, because "he had had the higher education portfolio and knew community colleges better than anybody, knew their budget better than anybody." Later, President Lancaster would hire Delores Parker, who had been chief academic officer at Guilford Tech and was a senior staffer at the Kellogg Foundation. Briggs and Parker would stay with Lancaster for his entire term, as would Ralls, except when he left to take the presidency of Craven Community College, partly to prepare for the day when he would apply for the system presidency. Before leaving, Scott recommended Larry Keen as his replacement, whom Lancaster hired. Keen would go on to become president of Fayetteville Technical Community College.

Other key administrators during the Lancaster years included Barry Russell, originally from Southwestern Community College, who was a Hackley hire but had only worked for him briefly at the end of his tenure, and who served as Hackley's and Lancaster's executive vice president. Russell would later be a finalist for head of the Kentucky Community College System and would eventually leave to become president at Midlands Community College and, later, head of the South Carolina Community College System. To replace him, Lancaster would hire Steve Scott from Southeastern Community College, who was a favorite of the presidents across the state. Lancaster stated, "The executive VP's number-one job is interfacing with the presidents, so I always hired somebody that they liked. So I brought in Steve Scott, who was wonderful.... He was with me about two years but really missed the campus and wanted to go back to being campus president, which I could understand. He really has a heart for students." Lancaster would replace Scott with Fred Williams, from Robeson Community College, which he remembers as "one of the best things I did in my eleven years." He states that Williams was "an absolute prince" and "a great community college administrator. He, as a very young person, had traveled all over the state with Dr. Ready, as sort of his driver. He was just an incredible guy with an incredible background in community colleges."

This leadership team would help Lancaster shepherd the community college system through what some would see as the golden years. President Lancaster, a native North Carolinian and certainly someone who believed strongly in the Herring philosophy of total education, worked tirelessly to ensure the promise of the community college system of a better life available to all. He would remind his audience during one of his early addresses after being named president, given at James Sprunt Community College in May 1998, "Education is, of course, more than just insurance against unemployment. As I said in my inaugural address last fall, we must never assume that workers who are technically trained to work in our businesses and industries do not also need a broad background in the arts and humanities. They are not automatons trained simply for efficient production, but they are citizens and members of society who deserve to share in its cultural and intellectual gifts as well as its economic benefits." He never lost sight of that promise.

Toward the end of Lancaster's first year in office, on May 4, 1998, Governor Hunt proposed a $12.9 billion budget for FY 1998–99. His education budget included $60 million for community colleges, including a 4 percent salary increase for teaching faculty, a 2 percent teaching-excellence bonus for outstanding faculty, a 1 percent bonus for nonteaching faculty/staff, and additional resources for technology, training programs for new and expanding industry, and enrollment increases. In the end, the legislature would approve a 3 percent increase for all community college personnel and $20 million for equipment and technology upgrades. They also provided funding so that faculty could qualify for a 2 percent performance bonus.

In his final State of the State address, given in Raleigh on February 1, 1999, Governor Hunt challenged North Carolina and its education system, "Let's set a bold course for North Carolina at the beginning of a new century. Let's set the goal of becoming first in education in America by 2010. Let's resolve to give every single child the chance to realize the full measure of their potential and their dreams. Let's secure, for every one of them, the promise that is North Carolina." Two weeks later, the governor announced that his budget put "two-thirds of our new resources to education, to keep us on track to becoming first in America by 2010." The budget included money to raise community college and university salaries by 3 percent and additional reserves that were slated for future salary increases. The General Assembly again supported the governor's desire to raise the salaries, passing a 3 percent salary increase and allowing community college faculty to qualify for a 2 percent bonus. The increases would help the system retain its faculty and recruit more effectively in the years ahead.

The following year, Hunt and other state leaders campaigned to provide funding for facilities at the community colleges and universities through state bonds. On September 22, 2000, he called on the American Federation of Labor–Congress of Industrial Organization union leaders and members at their forty-third state convention in Raleigh to support the bonds. He stated, "Facilities are not keeping pace with demand. Community colleges are bursting at the seams with long waiting lists for classes due to lack of space, and demand is only going up." Hunt pointed out that universities and community colleges projected a 30 percent increase in enrollment, an additional 100,000 students, over the next decade. To help colleges deal with this increase, the bonds, which were on the November ballot, provided for $2.5 billion for new construction and renovation at the universities and $600 million for the community colleges.

Martin Lancaster remembered that the bond referendum was critical to the community colleges, and indeed all of education, in the decade that followed. In the beginning, Lancaster said, the community colleges were not involved. The universities had sought a bond referendum, but polling indicated that the bond would not pass and the legislature was lukewarm in its support of the idea. According to Lancaster, university officials approached the community college system, stating, "We'd like for you to have a piece of the action to get this bond referendum passed." As Lancaster would later recall, "And since we'd never had any, 600 million sounded like a lot. So we quickly put together a list of priorities for all the colleges and put together a package and gave it to the legislature for 600 million.... Everyone got a building, some got more than one." Lancaster stated that community colleges generated strong business support for the bonds, with Phil Kirk as president of Citizens for Business and Industry and George Little, an insurance executive and community college trustee who had served in the Holshouser administration, providing leadership and direction. One of Kirk's lieutenants, Leslie Bevacqua, became campaign director for North Carolinians for Educational Opportunity, the committee that promoted the bond issue across the state. Lancaster said that Bevacqua had been Governor Hunt's appointment secretary, and with more than four hundred state boards and commissions in North Carolina, "She knew everyone in the state. We raised 2 or 3 million dollars very quickly and ran a campaign." He also stated that Molly Broad, the president of the university system who had replaced C. D. Spangler upon his retirement in 1997, understood that the community colleges were the key "and we worked really hard and well together. She and I traveled the state. We had rallies on many of our campuses, I think on all the university campuses, and she and I went to all of them. We worked really, really hard to pass it, as did all of our presidents and their boards of trustees and the board of governors at the university, and it passed." In fact, it passed by 81 percent of the vote, and every county in the state voted for it. It was the largest statewide bond referendum campaign for higher education in U.S. history.

Interestingly enough, former president Lancaster points out that if "we had waited six months, it would not have passed." He stated that the recession struck in 2001, the year after the bond referendum passed. What some people overlook, according to Lancaster, is that the $3.1 billion spread across the state was "an incredible economic stimulus. It put people back to work in every county [where there was a community college or university].... People went to work building, using that money. Second, because we were in a recession, every bid came in way under, and we built things, renovated things we didn't anticipate.... So it really was an incredible boost to our colleges and to the university."

Another initiative during the Lancaster years, which the bond referendum and Governors Hunt and Easley would support, was biotechnology. Governor Hunt and other state leaders had created the North Carolina Biotechnology Center in 1984, while Martin Lancaster was still in the General Assembly, and had made North Carolina a significant player nationally and internationally in biotechnology. Governor Hunt had convened an event in December 2000 at the North Carolina Biotechnology Center to announce a new North Carolina Genomics and Bioinformatics Consortium, which would unite at least eleven universities, sixteen corporations, and nine nonprofit institutions throughout North Carolina. Hunt announced, "The consortium will encourage these entities to share information and resources, plan strategic initiatives, and form alliances. North Carolina is breaking new ground with this consortium. It is a nationally unique effort." Most of the people at the conference felt that the university would be the critical educational partner, but a handful of community college personnel in attendance realized that there was going to be a need for a more robust workforce to support the growing biotechnology industry. And according to Lancaster, the university people thought that "anyone who worked in biotechnology needed to have a BS"—a bachelor of science degree. Lancaster and his team saw things differently. He remembered that they hired Stuart Rosenthal to do an independent study. With funding from the Golden Leaf Foundation, a foundation created by money from the settlement between the states and Big Tobacco, Rosenthal "interviewed hundreds of biotechnology people in this state, all over the country and internationally. It was a credible study looking at what you would need for a workforce in terms of skills and how you would develop those skills. The first conclusion that he reached was that two-thirds of the workforce did not need a BS, but needed education beyond the high school, preferably a two-year degree, but not necessarily a two-year degree." The Rosenthal survey indicated that approximately 67 percent of biomanufacturing jobs would require training and education at the community college level, and that in the next three years alone, biomanufacturing companies in the state would seek to hire more than six thousand employees. Lancaster points out that Rosenthal's study provided the impetus for Joanne Steiner, director of business services at Novozymes North America in Franklinton, to fund the development of a community college–based biomanufacturing training program, a six-week program that took workers from outside biotechnology and gave them the rudimentary skills they needed to be biotech workers. Lancaster stated, "It took off like a rocket. Before long, half or more of our colleges were offering it. We were demonstrating what Stuart had said: that for many of the jobs you didn't even need a two-year degree."

Lancaster ended up promoting Susan Seymour to the directorship of the community college system's BioNetwork program, an economic development initiative modeled on Steiner's and Seymour's earlier work, launched in August 2003 through funding by the Golden Leaf Foundation. The $60 million grant from the Golden Leaf Foundation went to train and retool workers for jobs in the growing biotech and pharmaceutical industries. Seymour, who had left the Department of Commerce in 1998, where she had been a program compliance manager and coordinator specializing in biotech, to become the regional training director for the North Carolina Community College System in the Research Triangle Region, helped author the grant request. Lancaster remembers that the grant further developed curriculum including two-year degrees and eventually "we got 63 million dollars, most of which was to build BTEC, the Golden Leaf Biomanufacturing Training and Education Center on Centennial Campus, which was the first joint use community college–university building. With our having a role below the BS level of education and their doing the BS and masters, it has full-scale technology equipment so that workers can go directly into jobs having experience on full-scale equipment." Lancaster remarked that Seymour was "tough as nails and she stood her ground [when confronted by university personnel who felt that community colleges could not play a substantial role in biotech], and ultimately we built the building and developed joint programs." As to the success of the program itself, Lancaster points out, "We went from seventh to third in the nation as a biotech state during the time that we took this initiative; passing Massachusetts and California was next to impossible. California would be the seventh-largest economy in the world if it were a country."

Another hallmark of the Lancaster presidency was the close working relationship that he developed with the new president of the university system,

Erskine Bowles. Not since Bill Friday and Dallas Herring had the leaders of the two systems worked so closely and so well together. Bowles had been elected by the universities' Board of Governors to succeed Molly Corbett Broad on October 3, 2005. Over the next two years, Lancaster and Bowles would work closely together to advance the cause of higher education in North Carolina. Lancaster remembers,

> God blessed us in the state when Erskine was hired as president. I had planned to retire after ten years, but Erskine and I were working on some things that we wanted to get institutionalized, and so I stayed on for another year. So that's why I served eleven instead of ten years. But what a great leader he was. The community college system benefited almost as much from his leadership as the university system did, because he was such a partner with me and with the system and pushed the university in ways that no academic administrator like Molly would have ever done.... He overcame a lot of inertia that had held back the relationship between the two.

Lancaster stated that Bowles was never in the thrall of the faculty and their committees the ways that some administrators were, and he would not countenance their sometimes long and drawn-out deliberative process. In March 2007 Lancaster announced that he would retire as system president in the spring of 2008. But he and others had an eye on a young leader at Craven Community College who had formerly worked for him, and who he was certain would make an excellent system president.

Lloyd V. Hackley, NCCCS President, 1995-1997

H. Martin Lancaster, NCCCS President, 1997-2008

Hilda Pinnix-Ragland, Chair, North Carolina State Board of Community Colleges, 2005-2013 (First Female and First African American Chair of the State Board)

R. Scott Ralls, NCCCS President, 2008–Present

Using the card catalog in the library at Isothermal Community College, 1984

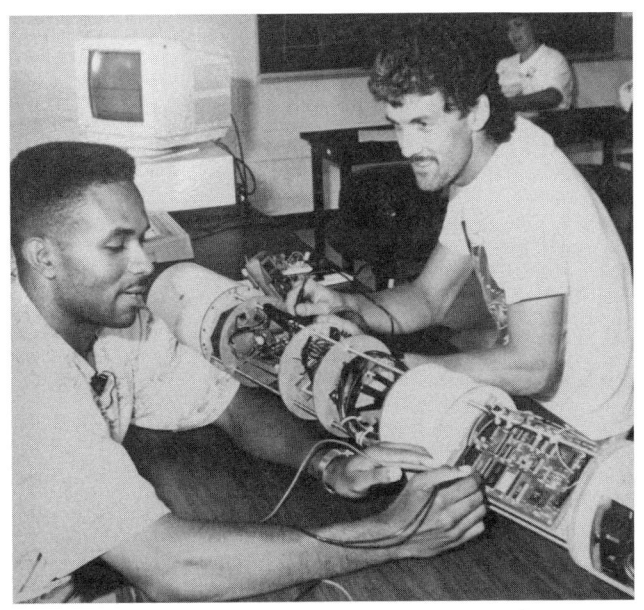

Engineering technology students construct a rocket at Southeastern Community College, 1991

Epilogue

There is one thing I am very sure about—we are the ones that North Carolina needs right now. We are the ones that thousands of North Carolinians have been waiting for. Why? Because we are North Carolina's cavalry, and in a North Carolina rocked by economic turmoil, we better strap in tight, because we have to give our jobs—the most important jobs that anyone could have right now—their closest attention. But as our state's economic cavalry, we also have to have North Carolina's attention. Because one thing I learned from watching movies as a boy is that the cavalry needs soldiers and horses to come to anyone's rescue.

SCOTT RALLS

I strongly believe that an educated workforce is much better than an uneducated one. And regardless of where they came from or how they got here, it is our job to educate them.

HILDA PINNIX-RAGLAND

R. Scott Ralls assumed the presidency of the North Carolina Community College System on May 1, 2008. Few people came better prepared by education or experience to lead a system of community colleges. Ralls was born in Charlotte, North Carolina, the son of a Methodist minister. He attended the University of North Carolina at Chapel Hill, where he obtained a bachelor of science degree in industrial relations. While at Chapel Hill, Ralls remembered working "at a little manufacturing company in Mount Airy. I worked on the assembly line, and I also worked in sales one summer, but mostly on the line." In those positions, he learned the importance of both organization and management.

After college he had the opportunity to go overseas as part of a Japanese business study program. While there he visited a huge Nissan automobile manufacturing facility in Yokohama, which, he recalled, didn't "seem to have many more workers than my little factory I had left in Mount Airy. They were maintaining equipment, programming equipment; they were not packaging like I had been doing by hand. I decided that day that what I was going to be interested in was more the workforce-training, human side of technologies."

Ralls returned to the States and enrolled in the University of Maryland, where he would earn a master of arts, followed by a PhD in industrial/organizational psychology. He continued to be interested primarily in the human side of technology, and his work with his advisors, who specialized in that area, led to a job in Washington, DC, working with the Department of Labor as a policy specialist analyzing the impact of technology issues, such as robotics, on the workforce. This led to a job with the U.S. Department of Commerce, as Ralls remembers, as "their workforce guy in technology areas." But home was calling, and as both he and his wife were from North Carolina, they moved back so that Ralls could take a job in Governor Hunt's Department of Commerce as the director of the Division of Employment and Training. He would serve in that role for about two years before joining the community college system.

Ralls left the Commerce Department to oversee customized training programs in the Department of Community Colleges and eventually became the Vice President of Economic and Work Force Development under Martin Lancaster. He left the system office to become the president of Craven Community College in 2002. In the six years that he was president of Craven, the college achieved record enrollment and fund-raising support. In addition, the college opened the Institute for Aeronautical Technology, developed the Bosch and Siemens Advance Manufacturing Center, and led the statewide redesign of information technology programs. Before leaving to return to Raleigh as system president, Ralls had also led the college in fostering unique educational partnerships, including a University Connections program with East Carolina University and N.C. State University's College of Engineering.

Ralls remembers that upon assuming the system presidency in the summer of 2008, he was immediately faced with two immediate challenges. He recalled, "I became president the first week of May that year, and by Thursday we found ourselves in the middle of what became a very big political issue, which was the issue about immigration and the admittance of undocumented students." President Ralls points out that in the end the board, and the system, went through a thoughtful, deliberate process that resulted in the decision to admit those students, while ensuring that North Carolina residents did not lose their place. In the end, it was a decision that was respected, though not everyone agreed with it. The second major challenge—which, to a lesser degree, the system faces even today—was the onset of economic recession. As he likes to tease his predecessor, "Lancaster was brilliant in that he somehow figured out how to retire the day the recession started in North Carolina. I don't know that May first of that year was the day that the recession started, but it was pretty darn close." As Ralls points out, in less than a year, the unemployment rate more than doubled. The end result was that the system was connected to the economy, and the rate of enrollment was tied to the fluctuation of jobs in North Carolina. As Ralls states, "For the first three years and certainly to this point, we were challenged with what became hypergrowth, the fastest-growing period in the history of our system. At the same time we probably faced the greatest budget challenges that our system has ever faced because of the revenue challenges that the state faced. So you combine those two things together, and that has certainly been the defining issue, the challenge during this time frame." But under the guidance of his steady hand, the North Carolina Community College System has not only survived but prospered. Indeed, today the fifty-eight community colleges in the system serve approximately 850,000 students each year. And the system is one of the largest systems of higher education in the United States, internationally recognized for its programs fostering economic and workforce development.

Few have said it better than Ralls's predecessor and mentor, H. Martin Lancaster. Soon after being chosen president of the North Carolina Community College System, Martin Lancaster was called upon to speak at a dedication of a new building at James Sprunt Community College in Kenansville, North Carolina. On that hot late-spring day, May 28, 1998, with his friend and mentor, Dr. Dallas Herring, in the audience, Lancaster paused to look back, even as he spoke of the opportunities that lay ahead. He reminded his audience,

Many of you were a part of those early years. You remember that today's system of fifty-nine institutions began as a handful of industrial education centers and a few two-year colleges with academic programs. Melding them into a strong system of comprehensive community colleges took years of careful planning, much negotiating with the General Assembly, and strong leadership, including the personal commitment of the late governor Terry Sanford. Virtually all the tributes to Governor Sanford following his recent death cited the creation of the system in 1963 as one of the most important accomplishments of his remarkable life in public service. How fortunate North Carolina was to have Terry Sanford at the helm, at this important juncture in our history, with Dallas Herring as his navigator, always showing the way to a brighter future for all North Carolinians, not just the select few who could afford an education in the liberal arts—pushing for an education that would combine the technical skills needed for the workplace with the exposure to the arts and humanities that would make the person whole.

This vision, like the Asbury flame to which Lancaster and others would refer in later speeches, would light the years that lay ahead for him and his generation. Hopefully, it will likewise shine brightly in the next fifty years of our history as well, lighting the pathway to success.

Afterword

R. Scott Ralls

Fifty years after the birth of North Carolina's community colleges, we the people of the open door—community college people—have accomplished milestones and gained momentum because we stand on the shoulders of audacious pioneers—leaders who dared to be so naïve as to imagine that access to higher education could be open to all North Carolinians, regardless of their income, their race, sex, or geography, and regardless of their previous academic preparation.

We are the product of audacious dreamers.

We are the product of Dr. Dallas Herring, the educational visionary who espoused the concept of "total education" and dreamed of a higher education system that could turn a naïve concept of postsecondary education for everyone into educational reality.

We are a product of Governor Luther Hodges, the economic visionary who dreamed of a workforce development system that could transform North Carolina from one of the poorest states in the nation to one recognized for its thriving diversification.

We are the product of Governor Terry Sanford, a political visionary who championed the long-term benefits of creating the most comprehensive community college system in the world, even in the face of the significant short-term sacrifices and challenges created by suggesting such a bold path.

And we are the product of Governor Bob Scott, who even after leading the state as governor noted that his time leading the North Carolina Community College System was his most fulfilling responsibility, because he saw and encouraged the power of community colleges to, in a transformational way, reach into all corners of North Carolina's diverse communities—urban and rural.

But most importantly, we are the product of thousands of educational pioneers—trustees, administrators, faculty, and students—who bought into a vision of improved prosperity from Murphy to Manteo through the novel concept of widely available education beyond high school.

"We must take the people where they are and carry them as far as they can go," said Dr. Herring, who in fewer than twenty words summarized the operating vision for North Carolina's community colleges. And it was the system pioneers who made that aspirational vision eventually reach one out of every eight adult North Carolinians, meeting the people where they entered but encouraging their aspirations to not be limited by any previous assumptions.

Just as North Carolina community college educators have for years encouraged our students to overcome self-limitations, it is vital at this threshold moment, fifty years after our system's birth and five years after the start of the Great Recession, for our system of open-door education to not be limited by the whispers of doubt.

As our system rounds the corner on its golden anniversary, it is doing so at a time of great economic challenge for our state. Fifty years after the system's creation, North Carolina is one of the most productive states in the nation with also one of the highest unemployment rates. North Carolina's population since the millennium has grown by almost 20 percent while the number of jobs in North Carolina has hardly grown. We are home to two of the fastest-growing cities in the nation as well as also some of the most economically depressed towns and counties. We have grown at twice the rate of the national average over the past ten years, but today one-third of our counties have death rates that exceed their birth rates.

At our fiftieth anniversary we also enter a period where doubt exists across the nation regarding the ability of the higher education sector to meet the great challenges of our day, to fulfill the promise of the American Dream that for so long rested on the coupling of educational and economic opportunity. Reports widely note the growing separate and unequal aspects of higher education, with low-income and working-class students increasingly concentrating in community colleges where the resource disparity gap widens compared to more "elite" colleges. Jeff Selingo, editor of the *Chronicle of Higher Education* and author of *College (Un)Bound*, referred to the 1999–2009 decade as the "Lost Decade" of higher education characterized by the guiding principle of more: "more buildings, more majors, more students, and of course, more tuition."

Leading into our fiftieth anniversary, community colleges found themselves most vulnerable to the criticism of not producing more graduates, in spite of great spikes in student enrollments. National leaders nervously noted the drop from the worldwide top spot to ninth in the percentage of young people graduating from college and the risks inherent for the long-term U.S. economy. President Barack Obama coined the phrase that America had reached its "new Sputnik moment" in a speech delivered at Forsyth Technical Community College in 2010.

When the Great Recession hit in 2008, it hit North Carolina particularly hard. Our system's enrollment soared, and our state's budget dropped. When we simultaneously faced the steepest enrollment climbs and the deepest budget cuts in our history, our system audaciously believed that still we could do things differently and better to help more students go from our registration lines to completing the journey across our graduation stages. And we did this at a time when it would have been very easy to say that we had plenty on our plate.

The collective efforts of North Carolina's community colleges to significantly increase student success at a time of economic hardship garnered a great deal of national attention, as illustrated by a quote from Bill Tucker of the Bill and Melinda Gates Foundation to our state board: "The eyes of the nation are upon you." And very importantly, fifty years after our creation, it captured the founding spirit of North Carolina's community colleges—a spirit of strength through diversity and strength through collective action to accomplish audacious, perhaps some would say naïve, goals in the face of significant challenge and adversity. A North Carolina spirit captured by Governor Terry Sanford over fifty years ago when arguing before the North Carolina General Assembly for the creation of a new state system of community colleges:

> You will hear some whisperings abroad saying that we have done enough, have moved well and far and rapidly, and so it is time now to slow down, rest, and catch our breath. These whispers come from the fearful and those who have always opposed the accomplishments from which they now would rest. This cannot be and is not the spirit of North Carolina.
>
> Much remains to be done, to provide better educational opportunities for the competition our children will surely face, to

encourage broader economic development so everybody will have a chance to make a better living. Now is the time to move forward. Now is no time to loaf along.

So after a remarkable fifty-year history since that quote was spoken, we have become the most comprehensive and accessible community college system in the world, a system characterized by doing the difficult. More than that, we have been tempered with the audacious examples of pioneering leaders, committed faculty and staff, and pathbreaking students who have demonstrated the values that the American Association of Community Colleges says will be required of all community college leaders in the future.

"Change cannot be achieved without committed and courageous leaders," notes the *21st-Century Commission on the Future of Community Colleges*. "Community colleges have been developing leaders to maintain the inherited design. They need now to develop leaders to transform the design."

Our challenge for the next fifty years—the challenge of our time for the North Carolina community college people, the people who open doors to opportunity and success—is do we have the audacity to believe in total education the way Dr. Herring and our philosophical forefathers did fifty years ago?

To make total education real, we must have the internal innovation and courage to believe that our higher education can be financially accessible to all North Carolinians in a way that also provides meaningful opportunity to all. We must believe that our higher education can be delivered with a rigor that worldwide competition demands and that we can support students in meeting those high thresholds, even when they come to us without benefit of strong previous preparation. We must also believe that our higher education can ensure that we give every student their very best shot at walking across a graduation stage with a credential of meaning—be it a degree, diploma, a certificate, or industry certification—when so many of them walked into our colleges facing some of life's most difficult challenges.

Access, excellence, completion—that is what total education demands today. It is also what our system of North Carolina community colleges have exemplified now for fifty years, and for a world at an economic crossroads I am convinced that it is a concept that today is more relevant than ever before.

I believe that our efforts to provide the open door to total education will define the future of our state. I just pray that we continue to have the audacity of spirit, exemplified by our pioneers, to meet the challenges of tomorrow.

"Beyond any question," said Dr. Herring during his 1964 address to the Orientation Conference on Community Colleges,

> the most significant achievement of this audacious adventure of the people of North Carolina, the most promising development and the event most worthy of remembrance in our history is the opening of the door to universal education beyond the high school, the door to total education, the door to unlimited learning for all of the people through the comprehensive community college system. The Community Colleges, the Technical Institutes, the Industrial Education Centers, by whatever name they are now called or will be called in the future, are the doorway through which the rank and file of North Carolina will march out of the past and into the mainstream of America.

R. Scott Ralls, President
North Carolina Community College System
Raleigh, North Carolina
September 9, 2013

Appendix A

"JUST A CITIZEN": EULOGY FOR WILLIAM DALLAS HERRING, DELIVERED ON JANUARY 9, 2007, AT MOUNT ZION PRESBYTERIAN CHURCH, ROSE HILL, NORTH CAROLINA

Joseph Wescott II, EdD

What shall we say then of William Dallas Herring? A man about whom so much has been said, so much written... A man, who when he was born, soldiers were fighting in the muddy trenches of World War I, horses were still the primary means of transportation in much of the United States, though you could buy a Model T for around five hundred dollars, and Woodrow Wilson, another Davidson scholar, was president. Born at 2 a.m. on March 5 in 1916 in the family home, just a few blocks from this church, Dallas Herring would live to see vast changes in this nation of ours, and in North Carolina he would play a leading role in many of those changes. Indeed, former governor Jim Holshouser said recently of him, "There is no question of his place in history."

Today, I would like to share with you a little of that history, but even more so, I would hope to share with you Dallas Herring, the man, as I knew him. I hope to do so without oversentimentalizing my subject, for Dallas would not be pleased if I did so. And I would hope to do so carefully, both in my choice of words and in my delivery, for he always delighted, as a graduate of Davidson, in correcting the grammar of a Wake Forest man. Those of you who knew him know what a great wordsmith he was and how meticulous he was in the use of the English language. I fondly remember him speaking a few years back at N.C. State and, after his speech, saying to a prominent North Carolina politician that I hoped to be able to speak like that when I was in my eighties, to which the House member responded, "I wish I could speak like that now."

In 1992, around the same time that Dallas and I met, he appeared on the program *North Carolina People* with his dear friend Dr. Bill Friday. Bill referred to him during that program as the finest manifestation of education statesmanship that North Carolina had seen in this (half) century. Dallas, after discussing some of the highlights of his forty-year career in education, said of himself, "I don't claim to be the fount of all wisdom; I am just a citizen who tried to help." And I think those words capture for us the man, Dallas Herring.

Just a citizen. From his earliest years, Dallas Herring demonstrated two traits that guided him throughout his career, a love of learning and a desire to share that with those less fortunate. Knowing that his hometown had no library, when he was in the sixth grade he established one in the local grocery store. That first library consisted of fifty to seventy books on loan from the state library. He maintained that library for several years, opening it each Saturday and checking out books to the public.

That love of books followed him throughout his life, and he told Bill Friday on *North Carolina People*, "I live in a house full of books." Of the thousands of books in his home today, three were always kept on the shelves closest to his chair: the New Testament in Greek, which he read often; *Memories of Davidson College*, by Walter Lingle, the man who was president when Dallas was there; and *The School That Built a Town*, by Walter Hines Page. It was Page, that eloquent Tar Heel journalist, who would influence Dallas Herring as much, if not more, than anyone. Dallas always enjoyed telling the story of when his parents, Burke and Lula Herring, took him to college in 1933. After they dropped Anne Louise and Sue by Flora Macdonald College, his mother and father stopped at Bethesda Church in Aberdeen. Though the church itself was locked, his mother searched the graveyard until she found Walter Hines Page's grave, for she wanted Dallas to see it. It is no surprise that one of the passages prominently marked in Page's book next to his chair reads, "We have often reminded ourselves and informed other people that we have incalculable undeveloped resources in North Carolina in our streams, our forests, our mines.... But there is one undeveloped resource more valuable that all of these, and that is the people themselves. It is about the development of men that I shall speak, more particularly about the development of forgotten and neglected men." Dallas Herring would come to firmly believe, with Page, that a system of public education was the only effective means to develop the forgotten men and women of this state.

How was it that this young bachelor, businessman, and successful local politician came to devote so much of his life to education? His eyes would twinkle when he would tell the story of how the members of the Duplin County Board of Education approached him twice to ask him to serve out the term of Robert Carr, who had been elected to the legislature in 1951. And twice he turned them down, feeling as he said that that was a job better served by someone with children of their own. But when they came back a third time and told him that they just could not find anyone else, he remembered, he said, "how the good Lord called Samuel three times and Samuel finally listened. Maybe God was trying to tell me something." Those of us who know of the marvelous career that followed have no doubt of Providence's hand in his selection.

Dallas was elected chairman of the Duplin County board at its first meeting and did such an outstanding job that he caught the eye of Governor Umpstead, who appointed him to the Pearsall Commission in 1954 to study the challenges confronting North Carolina as a result of the Supreme Court's ruling in *Brown v. Board of Education*. And in the following year Governor Umpstead's successor, Luther Hodges, appointed Dallas to the State Board of Education. He would serve on that board twenty-two years, the last twenty as its chairman. The rest, to use an overworn phrase, is history. In less than two years, he was pushing for the establishment of industrial education centers in North Carolina, which served as the genesis for the community college system. He oversaw a far-reaching curriculum study in the public schools and worked for increases in teacher pay, all the while receiving only $7.50 a month in reimbursement for his travel expenses. Insisting upon access for all to excellence, he superintended the desegregation and integration of the public schools. And as a member of the Board of Higher Education he played a key role in the expansion of the university system as well as in the creation of the community colleges.

During his long career, he served seven governors: Umpstead, Hodges, Sanford, Moore, Scott, Holshouser, and Hunt. Governor Scott, with whom Dallas was close, wanted very much to be here today, but for health reasons could not. Talking on the phone with him this weekend, Bob said of Dallas, "He was a mentor to me in public service. He gave an immense amount of his personal time and in his duties as chairman of the board, heaven only knows how many trips he made to Raleigh. For us youngsters, he was an excellent example of public service, in an area where it counted the most—education. I counted him as a friend, and he always had time to talk; indeed, he was the first person to have an open-door policy. He was quite willing to sit on the porch and talk." There were many of us who sat on that porch, if you will, and dined at that table. For another little-known fact was that Dallas Herring was a good cook and if you stayed long enough, you were certain to be asked to supper, and a fine southern meal it would be. During the early years of the community college system, visiting that porch and being approved by Dallas Herring was one of the final, but mandatory stops in the interview process for would-be college presidents.

Dallas Herring learned to cook from his mother, Lula. She and his twin sister, Sue, were the women in his life. He loved them both dearly, but not greatly more than the rest of his family. And I would say to the family today that I know that you were proud of him. But you may not know just how proud he was of you. I spent many evenings in front of the fire with Dallas Herring. And I always knew that we would discuss two things: the latest developments in the community college system and the latest additions to or achievements of the Herring or Southerland clans. You need only to visit his home and see, in addition to the vast holdings of books and genealogical records, the pictures hanging on the walls—whether it is his mother over the mantel or the pictures of nieces and nephews nearby—and you know, here was a man who understood the meaning of family.

In the later years of his life, in addition to painting, gardening, and writing, he continued to reach out to the forgotten and those on the fringes of society. Just two weeks ago I found affixed to the back door a card from a man in the Latino community named José, who had brought his family by to wish him a Merry Christmas and to thank him again for helping him complete his education at James Sprunt Community College. And it was Dallas Herring who, believing in the worth of all citizens, encouraged Delilah Gomes and the other ladies of Delta Sigma Theta to research and write the book *Legacies Untold: Histories of Black Churches in the Greater Duplin County Area*. It is no wonder that Martin Lancaster, the president of the community college system, referred to him as "North Carolina's renaissance man, the closest thing we have ever had to Thomas Jefferson."

For me he will always be the distinguished southern Christian gentlemen, in white shirt and black bow tie, sitting in front of the fire, extending his hand and saying, "Come on in and let's talk a while." I remember, it was during one of those evenings that he shared with me that it would be enough if it could be said of him at the end of his life, as Homer had written long centuries ago, "He was a friend to man, and he lived in a house by the side of the road." Dallas Herring, you were that and so much more...so much more.

Appendix B

FIFTY YEARS AND COUNTING... NORTH CAROLINA COMMUNITY COLLEGE SYSTEM GOLDEN ANNIVERSARY, GOLDSBORO, NORTH CAROLINA, SEPTEMBER 18, 2013

Benjamin Eagles Fountain Jr.

Fifty years, already! Time flies when you are having fun. Let's give Scott Ralls and Ed Wilson and their associates a standing ovation for arranging this splendid occasion. Thank you.

I trust you noticed my current title in the program. My earliest titles included mower of neighborhood lawns and newspaper carrier. I am truly grateful for this latest title here tonight. "Honorary chairman" carries with it notice but no work or responsibility. And the pay, of course, is commensurate. Some years ago I was pleased to be designated as a President Emeritus of the North Carolina Community System. Then I found that the translation of the Latin was, "Don't call us, we will call you." One is called "honorary chairman" when he has reached a seniority that suggests he is no longer likely to do anything to embarrass the program.

President Ralls asked me to talk about some of the founders and tell some stories of the early days of the system. As a carryover relic from the twentieth century I am qualified by time to do that. My memory has improved so much that I can even recall things that never happened. Longevity has its rewards.

We are here tonight to remember those who brought into being and nurtured the community college program in North Carolina. You will recognize their names: Dr. Allan Hurlburt of Duke University, who conducted a study showing such a program was needed in the state; Governor Luther Hodges, who led North Carolina into the modern era and created industrial education centers that with a handful of public junior colleges became the nucleus for the system; and Irving Carlyle, who led the Commission to Study Education Beyond the high School. John Saunders of Chapel Hill served as secretary to the commission and prepared the report that recommended a system of community colleges.

Dallas Herring, chairman of the State Board of Education, realized the time was ripe and set I. E. Ready and a team including Raymond Stone, Helen Dowdy, Gerald James, Fred Eason, and others to work drafting proposed community college legislation. The bill was introduced by Gordon Greenwood. Ed Wilson and Ned Delamar guided the community college bill through the House of Representatives in the 1963 General Assembly. Senate leaders included Lunsford Crew, vice chairman of the Carlyle Commission, Robert L. Humber, Tom White, and Ralph Scott. The State Board of Education named Dr. I. E. Ready as director of the new Department of Community Colleges. Governor Terry Sanford made certain that funding was available to launch the new program. Dallas Herring, the architect of the system, insisted that the colleges have local tax support, have local boards of trustees, be comprehensive in program offerings, and be open door to all. So here we are tonight—fifty years later—operating under the same structure and philosophy and doing quite well to the benefit of North Carolina citizens. Can you imagine a North Carolina without a community college system? The colleges are now the bone and sinew of the Tar Heel State.

Obviously I can only touch on just a few of the founders and their actions to create and build the system. There were hundreds more who played key roles. For more names and events I commend to you Kenyon B. Segner's *History of the Community College Movement in North Carolina, 1927–1963* and Jon Lee Wiggs's *The Community College System in North Carolina: A Silver Anniversary History, 1963–1988*. Also you will want to know that Ann Britt, Neill McLeod, and others have created an excellent timeline exhibit on the system history in the North Carolina Museum of History. Maybe that work could be put on tour someday. Neill McLeod was a true pioneer as the first female community college president in North Carolina.

What was it like in the early days of the system? It was a strikingly creative time. Harvard University was founded in 1636. The University of North Carolina opened its doors in 1795. The 1800s was the era of public elementary education. The late 1860s was the time of the land-grant college movement. The 1900s witnessed the rise of the high school and vocational education. Now in the second half of the twentieth century some of us had the privilege of building something new in education: the comprehensive two-year community college.

The citizens of the counties wanted fast results from their new colleges. Faculty members and administrators were quickly engaged. Arrangements were made for universities to accept our transfer students from the new and unaccredited colleges. I still recall my great relief when President Leo Jenkins of nearby East Carolina readily agreed to accept our students. The first Lenoir Community College catalog was published in the spring of 1966. We tried to see that a catalog was on the coffee table of every house in the county. One lady told me, "I could not believe we were really going to have a college until I saw the catalog." Many colleges began classes in old schools, abandoned jails, and storefronts. The county commissioners of Lenoir County provided us with money to renovate old World War II facilities at the airport. There we began classes while new buildings were constructed on the campus. BB&T provide a hot dog lunch for students on the opening day. When the move was made to the permanent campus we were swamped with students and parking problems. As I watched the gathering a young man came up to me and said, "You knew we were coming. Why weren't you ready?" We quickly converted a field of soybeans into a parking lot and reopened temporary class spaces at Stallings Field. Yes, we had a soybean field. We rented the land for a time for a nice sum and saved a ton on weed control and mowing. As we scrambled for space, a prominent lady approached me and said, "Do you like your job? If you do you better not mess up our sewing class." You can be sure all of the adult education classes and vocational programs were protected. We were on our way as a new comprehensive two-year college, and the same was happening across North Carolina.

One spring day a young man came by to apply for a faculty position teaching history. As we got acquainted he told me that he was going to marry Mable Smith, our college librarian. I asked him where they would live. He responded, "Wherever I get a job." Thinking fast I said, "You are hired." Mable Howell led the building of an outstanding library on the campus. Before moving on to bigger things, Bruce Howell introduced me to the mysteries of the stock market.

Soon Dallas Herring noticed an unseemly divisive competition among the colleges for limited state dollars. He designated a committee of presidents and others to work with Director I. E. Ready and Herman Porter, later a chairman of the State Board of Community Colleges, to develop a formula based on enrollment for the distribution of state appropriations. The competition diminished, and the colleges began to cooperate in the quest for state monies. More about that later.

Now fast forward to January 1971 and Raleigh. I had succeeded our founding director Dr. I. E. Ready and was sitting in his chair. For the first time since I was six years old I was not on a campus teeming with students and their teachers. There were no class-change bells ringing. There were offices up and down empty, bare-walled hallways with capable persons at work, but all was quiet. Helen Dowdy and others welcomed me with a beautiful cake and good wishes. A stream of employees led by John Blackmon came by to say hello and offer their resignations. I quickly put out the word for everybody to stay put and keep working. Other than remembering what I was missing on a campus, my major concern was wondering if my car was being towed by Raleigh's finest. A little before five o'clock I observed to Helen that it had been a pretty good first day and that I would leave. Right at five o'clock the telephone rang. The caller was a prominent citizen from a coastal community asking me to reverse a decision to allow his local college to expand its waterfront site. He was not happy when a few days later I told him the decision would stand. He never spoke to me again. And so it began.

In late winter that first year Reid Parrott came by to say that he was completing Edgar Boone's program of preparation of community college leaders at North Carolina State University and would like to work for the Department of Community Colleges. Founded at the urging of Dallas Herring, the program, complete with a peer-reviewed academic journal, became the model in the United States. I suggested that Reid come back after completing his doctorate. He did, and I was glad to get him as he brought to the department actual community college experience as a teacher and administrator. I told him, "I do not know how to hire someone for state government, but check around and tell someone I need you." He soon was back to say that he was on the payroll. I said, "Well, I do not know how to find you an office and secretary, but check around and get it done." And he did. To this day I do not know how he did it. By the end of the year when the department was reorganized into an academic format with a president rather than a director, he was named a senior vice president.

The legislature convened in early 1971. A young senator, Billy Mills, appeared in my office and stated that he wanted to help community colleges. Before the session ended he had obtained additional funds for the system.

In early 1973 Governor James Holshouser called for each college to get a basic construction grant of five hundred thousand dollars. Lieutenant Governor James Hunt agreed and showed his commitment by removing the cap of five hundred thousand dollars. Carl Stewart, Billy Mills, Ralph Scott, and others in the General Assembly went to work and by the end of the session had doubled the community system appropriations to $100 million. They were strongly backed locally by trustees such as Ed Stowe, Wallace Gee, Louis Shields, and Stacy Budd and presidents such as Woody Sugg and Dick Hagemeyer.

The system exploded with construction and enrollment. Vince Outland, our one person to oversee construction, put a hundred thousand miles per year on his car. Joe Carter and Carol Andrews facilitated the expansion of the college library collections to over 1 million volumes.

Now, about that funding formula. The chairman of the majority political party in the state and his local president dropped by unannounced to say that their college needed more money and wanted me to send some. I was not subjected to any pressure after explaining the funding formula. They went to work for more system funding.

The years of the seventies were a time of establishing new community colleges and converting technical institutes into colleges. The process included a local needs study, a commitment to provide local funding, approval by the state board, and action by the General Assembly. Led by Reid Parrott, Hugh Battle, Ike Southerland, Jane Mosley, Ann Britt, and Carol Andrews (Southerland) we attained a success rate of 100 percent. I remember well the Thursday afternoon when Ike Southerland and Reid Parrott on foot chased down a legislator's car on Jones Street as he was leaving for the weekend. That kind of commitment is beyond valuation. Terry Tollefson, chief executive of two other state community college systems, came to us by way of Duke University, bringing us a national perspective as he met the challenge of advanced planning theory then coming into practice. Lena Mayberry (Engstrom), expert teacher and linguist, joined us and wrote a biography of Dallas Herring while completing a doctoral degree.

On one occasion a legislator asked me in committee, if they approved the college under consideration, would I agree that this one would be the last? My response was that whenever a county submitted a proper study and the citizens agreed to tax themselves, I would bring it to the General Assembly. Before long he was at work for his own county college.

The community college system was established after the end of the era of statutory and de facto segregation. Nonetheless, Frank Byrd Weaver, Major Boyd, D. Boyer, and Marselette Morgan among their many other duties made certain that the colleges' doors were open to all and that student transfers to the traditionally black universities were enhanced. In 1980 Phail Wynn became the first black president of an institution.

The 1970s was a time of major change for the state's universities. For example, after a heated political struggle a medical school was established at East Carolina University. Eventually the public universities were brought together to be led by Bill Friday. I first met him—and Terry Sanford, too—in 1946 at Boys State in Chapel Hill. Young law students Bill and Terry were counselors. I worked closely with Bill Friday as we built the community college system and the university. One day in his office, after he was made responsible for oversight of the seventeen UNC constituent institutions, he told me of a problem that had just landed on his desk. How can I possibly look after so many universities? was his lament. "Bill," I blurted, "suppose you had about forty more colleges to oversee?" Scott, he never brought up the subject again.

Some legislators and others began to think that the system was beginning to stray from its job training mission. One day James Glenn of the business development arm of the Commerce Department visited to discuss the shortcomings of the community college system in the effort to recruit new industry to the state. He suggested that we visit the Technical Education Center in South Carolina to see the great job they were doing. I agreed and insisted that we make a stop in Charlotte to visit Central Piedmont Community College on the way home. Of course I was well acquainted with the fine South Carolina TEC program. Plus my uncle was chairman of the Greenville County Council and an ardent advocate of the Greenville center. Uncle Ed met us at the airport and escorted us on a campus tour of the impressive school. After a short hop to Charlotte we toured equally impressive Central Piedmont Community College. As we were leaving the General Aviation Terminal at RDU, a pensive Jim Glenn said, "Your program and Joe Sturdivant are fine. What you really need is money for training machinery and programs." He became a staunch ally.

The support of E. Michael Latta of the North Carolina Vocational Council was invaluable in dispelling the notion that we had lost our way. His perceptive reports and recommendations were invaluable guides for policy and actions.

The vocational and technical courses exploded in number during the 1970s, even as college transfer classes were added. Roger Worthington, Ken Oleson, Bobby Anderson, and Tony Bevaqua worked overtime in curriculum development to keep up with the demand. For example, Vercie Eller, a career nurse in the Department of Community Colleges, fostered a significant expansion of the nursing and allied health programs among the colleges. It was during her tenure that two-year nursing programs attained 100 percent passing rates on the state licensing examinations. I am told that today the community colleges are the major source for allied health personnel in North Carolina. Next time you are hospitalized, ask around. You will be grateful.

The expansion of advanced job training and college courses across the state stimulated the demand for adult and basic literacy education. Charles Barrett among others ensured that adult education was up to the challenge.

Literally hundreds of trustees, college presidents, and others pulled together to build out the system. The name index in Jon Wiggs's book on the first twenty-five years of the system lists some seven hundred people, and he wrote that there were more.

Over time the respective colleges developed individual specialties and programs responsive to local circumstances while being partners in a system. This is appropriate for community colleges.

The State Board took a broad view of what constituted job training. Some of the more interesting variations included watercolor painting, belly dancing, and crabmeat picking. Public ridicule soon wiped out several such programs or drove them underground. The training of volunteer firefighters continued under Keith Phillipi.

Aviation-related programs survived in the form of ground schooling, power, and frame classes. But pilot flight training was not permitted.

Dallas Herring would not fly. He and I were invited to visit the South Carolina Technical System, and they promised to pick us up and return us home in the state airplane. Dallas said tell them to send a mule and cart and we will go.

Many of the department personnel had never been on a community college campus. We made a field trip to Cape Fear Technical College so that they could see what they were helping to build. The visit was capped by a cruise on the college training vessel downriver to the ocean buoy. Dallas was the first to board the ship—but no airships!

President Clyde Erwin of Wayne Community College called me in Raleigh one day to say that his college had obtained an airworthy military surplus helicopter for mechanical training purposes. He wanted me to give him permission to send a local pilot to bring it to the campus. I reminded him of the no-fly policy, of which he was already well aware. Some days later I asked Clyde if he got his helicopter. He said yes and that his was the only school to pick up one by truck. "Next time I will ask forgiveness rather permission," he said.

By the fifteenth year of the system, each college was accredited and each had a permanent campus. The fifty-eighth and final college, Brunswick, was being planned. The creation of a State Board of Community Colleges, the transfer to the Department of fiscal affairs led by Tom King, and other major changes were yet to come.

Now, fast-forward again to a happy ending. I was back on a community college campus welcoming students and faculty members on opening day to a place of comprehensive education for adults. Many others from the department likewise were returning as leaders to the college campuses.

We had our beginning fifty years ago this year. We are now in our fifty-first year and counting. Under the leadership of state board chairman Hilda Pinnix-Ragland and her fellow board members and President Scott Ralls and his leadership team and fifty-eight presidents and hundreds of college trustees, we are on the way to an even greater second fifty years. Thank you for sharing my memories.

Benjamin Eagles Fountain Jr.
President Emeritus, NCCCS

Bibliography

UNPUBLISHED MATERIALS

Manuscript Collections

Bevaqua, Anthony J. Papers. Duplin County Historical Foundation Library. Rose Hill, North Carolina.

Herring, William Dallas. Papers. Special Collections Research Center. North Carolina State Universities Libraries, Raleigh, North Carolina.

Hodges, Luther H. Papers. North Carolina Archives. Raleigh, North Carolina.

———. Southern Historical Collection. Chapel Hill, North Carolina.

Interviews and Personal Communications

Bevaqua, Anthony J. Interview by author. Cary, North Carolina, November 30, 1998.

Delamar, Ned E. Community college reminiscences (recording). Oriental, North Carolina, March 4, 1996.

———. Interview by author. Oriental, North Carolina, November 23, 1998.

Dowdy, Helen. Interview by author. Cary, North Carolina, March 9, 1999.

Flowers, William L. Interview by Lena Mayberry. Duplin County Historical Foundation Library. Rose Hill, North Carolina.

Friday, William Clyde. Interview by author. Chapel Hill, North Carolina, January 14, 1999.

Hackley, Lloyd "Vic." Interview by author. Raleigh, North Carolina, November 7, 2012.

Hall, Dixon. Telephone interview by author. Wallace, North Carolina, November 28, 1998.

Hayes, R. Barton. Interview by author. Raleigh, North Carolina, March 4, 1996.

Henderson, David. Interview by author. Wallace, North Carolina, December 2, 1998.

Herring, William Dallas. Interviews by author. Rose Hill, North Carolina, April 3, 1997; April 25, 1997. April 21, 1999; July 6, 1999; Raleigh, North Carolina, March 4, 1996.

———. Interview by Jay Jenkins. Southern Oral History Program. University of North Carolina at Chapel Hill, February 14, 1987.

———. Interview by Sherman Hayes. Videotape. Duplin County Historical Foundation Library. Rose Hill, North Carolina. February 2, 1998.

Hurlburt, Allan. Interview by Lena Mayberry. November 22, 1971.

Hunt, James. Interview by author. Raleigh, North Carolina. September 25, 2012.

Morrissey, Sharon. Interview by author. Raleigh, North Carolina. September 13, 2012.

Rankin, Edward. Interview by author. Concord, North Carolina. June 4, 1998.

Ralls, Scott. Interview by author. Raleigh, North Carolina. September 11, 2012.

Scott, Robert. Conversation with author. Kenansville, North Carolina. July 28, 1995.

Stone, Raymond. Interview by author. Wallace, North Carolina. March 19, 1997.

———. Speech at North Carolina Community College Celebration. Videotape. Greensboro, North Carolina. June 4, 1999.

Theses and Dissertations

Batchelor, John. "Save Our Schools: Dallas Herring and the Governor's Special Advisory Committee on Education." Master's thesis, University of North Carolina at Greensboro, 1983.

Flowers, William L. "The Community Action Movement in North Carolina." EdD diss., North Carolina State University, 1970.

Hodges, Joseph Milton, Sr. "The Governor's Commission on Education beyond the High School: The Carlyle Commission 1961–1963." EdD diss., North Carolina State University, 1995.

Lochra, Albert Pultz. "The North Carolina Community College System: Its Inception—Its Growth—Its Legal Framework." EdD diss., University of North Carolina at Greensboro, 1978.

Mayberry, Lena P. D. "William Dallas Herring: Leader in Five Issues in Education in North Carolina, 1955–1965." EdD diss., North Carolina State University, 1972.

Smith, Kathryn Baker. "The Role of the North Carolina Community College System in the Economic Development of the State's Communities." EdD diss., North Carolina State University, 1996.

Wescott, Joseph. "Competing Visions: Herring and Hodges and the Conception of the Community College System in North Carolina." Master's thesis, North Carolina State University, 1998.

PUBLISHED MATERIALS

Books and Journal Articles

Bass, Jack, and Walter De Vries. *The Transformation of Southern Politics: Social Change and Political Consequence since 1945*. New York: Basic Books, 1976.

Byerly, Victoria. *Hard Times Cotton Mill Girls: Personal Histories of Womanhood and Poverty in the South*. Ithaca, NY: ILR Press, 1986.

Dougherty, Kevin J. *The Contradictory College: The Conflicting Origins, Impacts, and Futures of the Community College*. Albany: State University of New York Press. 1994.

Flowers, Linda. *Throwed Away: Failures of Progress in Eastern North Carolina*. Knoxville: University of Tennessee Press, 1992.

Gleazer, Edmund J. "Evolution of Junior Colleges into Community Colleges." In *A Handbook on the Community College in America: Its History, Mission, and Management*. Ed. George A. Baker III. Westport, CT: Greenwood Press, 1994.

Gordon, Howard R. *The History and Growth of Vocational Education in America*. Needham Heights, MA: Allyn and Bacon, 1999.

Hall, Jacquelyn D., James Leloudis, Robert Korstad, Mary Murphy, Lee Ann Jones, and Christopher B. Daly. *Like a Family: The Making of a Southern Cotton Mill World*. Chapel Hill: University of North Carolina Press, 1987.

Hamilton, C. Horace. *Community Colleges for North Carolina: A Study of Need, Location, and Service Areas*. Raleigh: North Carolina State College, 1962.

Herring, William Dallas. *What Has Happened to the Golden Door?* Rose Hill, NC: Bedwyr Historical Press, 1992.

Hodges, Luther H. *Businessman in the Statehouse: Six Years as Governor of North Carolina*. Chapel Hill: University of North Carolina Press, 1962.

Kerr, Janet C. "From Truman to Johnson: *Ad Hoc* Policy Formulation in Higher Educations." In *ASHE Reader on the History of Higher Education*, ed. Lester F. Goodchild and Harold S. Wechsler, 628-652. Needham Heights, MA: Ginn Press, 1989.

Lange, Alexis F. "The Junior College as an Integral Part to the Public School System." *School Review* 25 (September 1, 1917): 465–79.

Leloudis, James L. *Schooling the New South: Pedagogy, Self, and Society in North Carolina, 1880-1920*. Chapel Hill, University of North Carolina Press, 1996.

Link, William. *The Paradox of Southern Progressivism, 1880–1930*. Chapel Hill: University of North Carolina Press, 1996.

Miller, Leonard P. *Education in Buncombe County, 1793–1965*. Asheville, NC: Miller Printing Co., 1965.

Mitchell, Memory F., ed. *Addresses and Public Papers of James Baxter Hunt Jr., Governor of North Carolina*. Vol. 1, *1977–1981*. Raleigh: North Carolina Division of Archives and History, Department of Cultural Resources, 1982.

———. *Addresses and Public Papers of James Eubert Holshouser Jr., Governor of North Carolina, 1973–1977*: Raleigh, North Carolina Division of Archives and History, Department of Cultural Resources, 1978.

———. *Addresses and Public Papers of Robert Walter Scott, Governor of North Carolina, 1969–1973*. Raleigh: North Carolina Division of Archives and History, Department of Cultural Resources, 1974.

———. *Messages, Addresses, and Public Papers of Daniel Killian Moore, Governor of North Carolina, 1965–1969*. Raleigh: State Department of Archives and History for the Council of State, 1971.

———. *Messages, Addresses, and Public Papers of Terry Sanford, Governor of North Carolina, 1961–1965*. Raleigh: Council of State, 1966.

Page, Walter H. *The School That Built a Town*. New York: Harper and Brothers, 1952.

Patton, James W., ed. *Addresses and Papers of Governor Luther Hartwell Hodges, Governor of North Carolina, 1954–1961*. 3 vols. Raleigh: Council of State, 1963.

Poff, Jan-Michael, ed. *Addresses and Public Papers of James Baxter Hunt Jr., Governor of North Carolina*. Vol. 3, *1993–1997*. Raleigh: Division of Archives and History, Department of Cultural Resources, 2000.

———. *Addresses and Public Papers of James Grubbs Martin, Governor of North Carolina*. 2 vols. Raleigh: Division of Archives and History, Department of Cultural Resources, 1992–1996.

Poff, Jan-Michael, and Jeffrey J. Crowe, eds. *Addresses and Public Papers of James Baxter Hunt Jr., Governor of North Carolina*. Vol. 2, *1981–1985*. Raleigh: North Carolina Division of Archives and History, Department of Cultural Resources, 1987.

Poff, Jan-Michael, and William H. Brown, eds. *Addresses and Public Papers of James Baxter Hunt Jr., Governor of North Carolina*. Vol. 4, *1997–2001*. Raleigh: North Carolina Division of Archives and History, Department of Cultural Resources, 2008.

Powell, William S. *Dictionary of North Carolina Biography*. 4 vols. Chapel Hill: University of North Carolina Press, 1979.

———. *North Carolina through Four Centuries*. Chapel Hill: University of North Carolina Press, 1989.

Sanford, Terry. *But What About the People?* New York: Harper and Row, 1966.

Segner, Kenyon Bertel, III. *A History of the Community College Movement in North Carolina, 1927–1963*. Kenansville, NC: James Sprunt Press, 1974.

Thornton, James W. *The Community Junior College*. New York: Wiley, 1972.

Tollefson, Terrence A. "The Evolution of State Systems of Community Colleges in the United States." In *A Handbook on the Community College in America: Its History, Mission, and Management.*, ed. George A. Baker III, 74–89. Westport, CT: Greenwood Press, 1994.

Wiggs, Jon Lee. *The Community College System in North Carolina: A Silver Anniversary History, 1963–1988*. Raleigh: North Carolina State Board of Community Colleges, 1989.

Newspapers and Magazines

Asheville Citizen and Times, August 31, 1961–October 1, 1962.
Charlotte Observer, April 21, 1953—November 27, 1959.

Greensboro Daily News, January 4, 1958—September 17, 1961.
Goldsboro News-Argus, February 17, 1952–January 31, 1959.
Leaksville News, November 6, 1958.
Raleigh News and Observer, February 17, 1952–July 21, 1961.
   Spotlight, January 1963.

Government Documents

Biennial Report of the State Superintendent of Public Instruction, 1950–1952. Raleigh, 1952.

Census Data: 1950, North Carolina. U.S. Bureau of the Census. Washington, DC, 1952.

The Community College Connection. Raleigh: Department of Community Colleges.

Dimensions of Poverty in North Carolina. Raleigh: North Carolina Fund, 1963.

"Education in North Carolina Today and Tomorrow." Report of the State Education Commission. Raleigh: United Forces for Education, 1948.

Four Speeches. Raleigh: Department of Community Colleges, January 1969.

Hurlburt, Allan S. *Community College Study*. Raleigh: State Superintendent of Public Instruction, 1952.

IEC: A Guide to the Further Development of Industrial Education Centers in North Carolina. Raleigh: Department of Curriculum Study and Research, 1963.

Industrial Training for High School Youth and Adults Offered by Industrial Education Center, Burlington, North Carolina, Bulletin 1. Burlington: Industrial Education Center, 1959.

Journal of the Senate of the General Assembly of the State of North Carolina, 1957 Session. Raleigh.

Latta, E. Michael. *The North Carolina Story: Knowledge APPLIED Is Power!* Raleigh: State Advisory Council on Vocational Education, 1990.

North Carolina Board of Education. Minutes of the State Board of Education. Raleigh.

North Carolina Board of Higher Education. *Biennial Report for 1957–1959*. Raleigh, 1959.

───. *Biennial Report of the North Carolina Board of Higher Education, 1961–1963.* Raleigh, 1963.

───. *Biennial Report of the North Carolina Board of Higher Education, 1963–1965.* Raleigh, 1965.

───. Minutes of the North Carolina Board of Higher Education. Raleigh.

North Carolina Public School Bulletin. Raleigh: State Department of Public Instruction.

Progress Report of the Community College System of North Carolina: First Five Years, 1963–1968. Raleigh: State Board of Education, 1969.

Progress Report: North Carolina Community College System, 1958–1971. Raleigh: Department of Community Colleges, October 6, 1971.

Regulations Governing the Establishment of Industrial Education Centers. Raleigh, 1958.

Report of the President's Commission on Higher Education for Democracy, 1947. Washington, D.C.

State Board of Education Brief Submitted to the Joint Committee on Appropriations. Raleigh, March 26, 1959.

Index

A

Advisory Budget Commission, 25, 29, 38, 100, 101
Adult Basic Education (ABE), 79, 105, 115
Act to Promote and Encourage Education Beyond the High School (Omnibus Education Act of 1963), 60
African American(s): students, 4, 34, 120, 121, 125; leadership from, 84, 101, 111, 115, *134i*, 140, 154; See also Black, Minority, Race
Archie, William (State Board of Higher Education), 52
Anson (Ansonville): extension unit, 45; IEC, 59
Articulation agreement, 82, 142-143
Asheboro IEC: site, 29
Asheville-Biltmore College, 14, 52
Asheville-Buncombe Technical Community College, 67
Asheville IEC: site, 29
Asheville Junior College, 4 22, 62, 66

B

Barden, Graham, 32-33
Bevaqua, Anthony "Tony" J., 45, 179
Black(s): leadership, 102, 178; personnel, 125; students, 125; tenant farmers, 5; voters, 72; universities, 178; See also African Americans, Minority, Race
Blake, Larry J. (NCCCS President), 111-114, 11-17, 119, 121-122, *134i*
Boone, Edgar J. (Adult and Community College Education, NCSU), 79-80, 90, 104, 106, 108, *134i*
Bowles, Erskine, (President, University of North Carolina System), 153
Boyles, Harlan, 116, 118, 119
Briggs, Kennon, 147
Broughton, J. Melvin, Junior, 83-4
Brunswick Technical Institute, proposal for, 110; 115, 180
Bruton, H. David, 107-109, 116

C

Caldwell Community College and Technical Institute, 92, 94, 128
Caldwell Technical Institute, 82, 89
Cape Fear Community College, *96i*, 130, 180
Caldwell, John T., 122
Carlyle, Irving, 1, 50, 53, 56, 62, 173; Carlyle Commission (Governor's Commission on Education Beyond the High School), 50- 52, 54, 55, 58-59, 62, 174; Commission Report, 60
Carteret Community College, *68i*
Carteret Technical College, 127
Catawba Technical Institute, 109
Catawba Valley Community College, *40i,* 124
Central Carolina Technical College, 121, 146
Central Carolina Technical Institute, 105
Central Piedmont, 45
Central Piedmont Community College, 76, 82, 106, 121, 124, 127, 132, 178
Chappell, Sidney, 30
Charlotte College, 52, 61, 66
Charlotte IEC: site, 29, 33
Charlotte Junior College, 4, 22, 48, 62, 66
Cherry, R. Gregg (Governor), 3, 10, 11
Chesson, Parker, 142
Cleveland Technical Institute, 77
Coastal Carolina Community College, 128
College of the Albemarle, 52, 66, 115, 127, 128
Commission on the Future of the North Carolina Community College System, 104, 106, 129-132, 139
Community College Act of 1957, 22, 23, 25, 48, 60, 66
Community College Advisory Council, 58, 60, 66, 108, 110
Community Colleges for North Carolina: A Study of Need, Location, and Service Areas, 52
Cone, Bonnie (Director, Charlotte College), 52, 61, 62, 66
Craven Technical Institute, 77, 81

Craven Community College, 147, 153, 158
Currin, Ben F., 105, 117

D
Davidson College, 18, 21, 100, 168
Davidson County Community College, 97i, 127
Davis, A. C., 59, 74-75
Delamar, Ned E., 46, 64, 145, 174
DelMastro, Salvatore, 61, 76
"Development of North Carolina Community College Planning Capabilities" Report, 103
Development of a System of Higher Education Committee, 52
Durham IEC: site, 29, 31, 33, 34
Durham Technical Institute, 45, 46, 94, 102, 115, 124, 134i, 147

E
Easley, Mike (Governor), 151
East Carolina College, 52
East Carolina University, 12, 90, 158, 178
Edgecombe IEC: site, 81
Erwin, Clyde Atkinson, 9, 10, 12, 14, 16, 180

F
Fayetteville IEC Site, 29
Fayetteville State University, 140-141
Fayetteville Technical Community College, 147
Fayetteville Technical Institute, 94, 105
Female(s): leadership, 134i, 154i, 174; students, 93, 115, 117
Focused Industrial Training, 131
Forsyth Technical Community College, 85i, 124, 163
Fountain, Benjamin E. (NCCCS President), 65, 78, 94, 96i, 99, 101, 103, 104, 108-110, 124; "Fifty Years and Counting," 173-180
Friday, William "Bill" C. (President, University of North Carolina System), 3, 49, 52, 57, 66, 120, 123, 132, 141, 153, 168, 178

G
"Gaining the Competitive Edge," 133
Gaston College, 97i, 124, 127, 128
Gaston Community College, 139
George-Barden Act of 1947, 8
G. I. Bill of Rights, 3, 8
Gill, Edwin, 24, 73-77
Gillespie, David, 114
Green, James "Jimmy" C., Jr., 107, 109, 111, 116

Greensboro IEC: site, 29
Greensboro Junior College, 4
Greenwood, Gordon, 64, 174
Golden Leaf Foundation, 151-152
Goldsboro IEC: site, 29; IEC, 32, 36, 43, 45
Governor's Commission on Education Beyond the High School (Carlyle Commission), 1, 50, 53
Governor's Commission on Workforce Preparedness, 138
Guilford County IEC, 31, 32
Guilford Technical Community College, 127, 131, 138, 146, 147
Guilford Technical Institute, 120, 127

H
Hackley, Lloyd "Vic" (NCCCS President), 137, 140, 141, 143, 144, 145, 147, 154i
Halifax IEC: site, 81
Hall, Dixon, 45, 76
Hamilton, Dr. C. Horace (Sociology, North Carolina State College), 52-53, 55, 62
Hawkins, Reginald, 84
Hayes, R. Barton, 20-21, 87, 107, 109
Haywood Technical Institute, 77
Helms, Jesse, 55-56
Henderson, David, 33
Herring, William Dallas, 1, 2, 4, 5, 16i, 17-34, 36-40, 42-44, 49-51, 54, 56-66, 69, 72-81, 83, 87, 91, 94, 100-107, 114, 123, 129, 132, 137, 148, 153, 159-162, 164, 167, 168, 170-171, 174-177
Higher Education Commission, 21
Hill, Watts, 25, 33-34
Hodges, Luther Hartwell (Governor), 17-21, 23-27, 32-33, 36-39, 41, 60-61, 63, 81, 87, 161, 169, 173
Hollings, Ernest F., 50
Holloman, Charles R. (NCCCS President, interim), 110, 112
Holshouser, James E. (Eubert), Jr. (Governor), 95, 99-104, 111, 123, 129, 150, 167, 169, 177
Holt, Bertha, 112
Hough, John, 36, 63-64
Humber, Robert Lee, 61, 65, 174
Hunt, James "Jim" B., Jr. (Governor), 99-100, 105-109, 111-118, 122-124, 126, 135i, 137-8, 140, 145, 148-149, 151, 169, 177
Hurlburt, Allan S. 12-14, 19, 21, 39, 52, 66; Hurlburt Commission, 12, 173; Hurlburt Report, 14, 29

I

Industrial Advisory Panel, 26
Isothermal Community College, 109, *155i*
Isothermal IEC; site, 45, 59

J

James Sprunt Community College, 114, 148, 159, 170
James Sprunt; extension unit (Goldsboro IEC), 45
James Sprunt IEC, 59
James Sprunt Institute, *68i*
James Sprunt Technical Institute, 76
James, Gerald, 43, 47-48, 51, 59, 108
Jenkins, Leo (President, East Carolina College), 52, 90, 175
Jobe, L. H., 12, 25
Johnston Community College, 45, 89
Johnston Technical College, 121
Johnson Technical Institute, 89

K

Kiser, Roger, 15

L

Lake, I. Beverly, 39, 71-72
Lancaster, H. Martin (NCCCS President), 137, 145-152, *154i*, 158-160, 170
Lange, Alexis F., 7
Larkins, John D., 39
Lenoir Community College, *40i*, 94, 127, 175
Literacy, 36, 128, 141, 179

M

Martin Community College, 113, *134i*
Martin, James G. (Governor), 126-129, 133
Martin, Wade (Director, Industrial Education Centers), 27-29, 31-32, 35-37, 43, 47, 50-51, 91
McDowell Technical Institute, 93
McCrary, Charles "Charlie" W., 20, 26-27, 31-32, 37, 42-44, 50, 63
McLendon, Major L. P., 48-49, 52
McLeod, C. Neill (President, Martin Community College), 113, *134i*, 174
Military, 33, 105, 128, 180
Mills, William "Billy" Donald, 108, 112, 123, 176-177
Minority(ies): enrollment, 93, 102, 115; leadership by, 102, 113; population, 4; race, 113; See also African American, Black

Montgomery (County): site for technical institute, 81
Morrisey, Sharon, 141-2
Moore, Dan (Governor), 67, 69-73, 76, 77, 80-84, 87, 120, 169

N

Nash: site for technical institute, 81
Nash Technical College, 130
National Commission on Teaching and America's Future, 145
New Hanover IEC, 31-32
North Carolina Biotechnology Center, 151
North Carolina State College, 36, 52
North Carolina State University, 80, 90, 92, 104, 108, 117, 122, 138, 158, 168, *134i*, 176
Nursing, 67, *68i*, 82, 128, 179

O

Obama, Barak, 163
Omnibus Education Act of 1963 (Act to Promote and Encourage Education Beyond the High School), 60
Open Door, The, 72, 76, 79, 82, 91

P

Pamlico Extension Unit (Goldsboro IEC), 45, 46, 74
Pamlico IEC, 59, 75
Pamlico Technical College, 121
Pamlico Technical Institute, 105
Pearsall Commission, 169
Phillips, A. Craig, 63, 105-107
Phillips, Guy, 21, 23, 63-64
Pinnix-Ragland, Hilda (Chair, State Board of Community Colleges), *154i*, 157, 180
Pitt Community College, 89, *135i*
Pitt IEC, 45, 59
Pitt Technical Institute, 105
Porter, Herman, 75, 175
Porter, J. D., 105
Preyer, Richardson, 67, 70-72
Purks, Harris, 22-23, 48

R

Race, 34, 39, 72, 113, 117, 161; racial discrimination, 4, 110; racial distribution, 110, 117; racial tension, 33; see also African America, Black, Minority

Ralls, R. Scott (NCCCS President), 137, 147, 154i, 157, 158, 159, Afterword 161-165, 173, 180
Ramsey, D. Hiden, 21-23, 29-30, 49
Rankin, Ed, 17-18, 70-71
Ready, I. E. (Isaac Epps), (NCCCS President), 16i, 59-60, 63, 65-66, 72, 75-76, 87, 89, 91-94, 123, 148, 174-76
Ready Award, 123
"Revised North Carolina State Plan for the Further Elimination of Racial Disparity in the Public Education System, Phase II: 1978-83," 110
Robeson Community College, 148
Robeson Technical Institute, 77
Rose, Charles, 20-21, 63

S
Sanders, John, 51, 59,
Sanford, Terry (Governor), 39-41, 45-49, 55, 57-67, 70-72, 79-81, 87, 107, 113, 117, 123, 160-161, 163, 169, 174, 178
Scott, Ralph, 11, 174, 177
Scott, Robert W. (Governor, NCCCS President), 41, 70, 83-84, 87-89, 91, 94-95, 100, 111-112, 121-132, 134i, 140-142, 161
Scott, Steve, 148
Seawell, Malcolm, 39
Smith, Bud, 55
Smith, J. Warren, 13, 23-24, 28
Smith-Hughes Act of 1917, 7
Soldiers and sailors, 4
Southwestern Technical Institute, 93
Spangler, C. D. (Clemmie Dixon "Dick"), 140, 141, 144, 150
Spikes, L. E., 34
State Board of Community Colleges (SBCC), 107, 114, 116-117, 120-123, 127-129, 146, 175
State Board of Higher Education, 21-24, 26, 48-49, 52, 66, 82, 169
State Education Commission, 11
Stone, Raymond, 1, 49, 59, 101, 121, 174
Sugg, Woody, 63, 177

T
Tart, John L., 45, 46, 108, 110, 113, 121-122
Taylor, Roy, 14; Taylor Bill, 15-16
Technical Institute of Alamance, 93
Thornburg, Murray, 27
Truman, Harry, 8; Truman Commission, 8, 14

U
Umstead, William B., (Governor), 17-21, 169
University of North Carolina (Chapel Hill), 3, 10, 18, 21-22, 36, 41, 49, 52, 100, 120, 145, 157, 174; Faculty Club, 58; Government Executives Institute, 140
"Upgrading Minorities: Patterns and Trends, 1970 to 1978," 110

V
Valentine, Ivan, 51
Valentine, Tim, 77
Vance-Granville Community College, 117, 124
Veterans, 2, 3, 96i; see also soldiers and sailors
Wynn, Phail, Junior (President, Durham Technical Institute), 115, 178, 134i

W
Waggoner, William, 63-64
Wake Technical Institute, 107
Watkins, William T., 130
Wayne Community College, 89, 180
Wayne Technical Institute, 73-74, 81
Wilmington College, 48, 52, 62, 66
Wilmington Junior College, 4, 22, 62, 66
Wilson, Edward H., Junior, 64, 73, 117, 124, 173, 174
Wilson, Edward H., Senior, 124
Wilson, Woodrow, 7, 167
World War II, 2, 7, 118, 175

Z
Zook, George F., 8; Zook Commission, 8; Report, 10